Fall In Love With Life

Donna Higton

Dedication

For everyone who *knows* there is more to life.

Acknowledgements

Thank you to the many, many people who helped me to write this book. Special thanks must go to Flymo, who read the first half of the book from cover to cover and filled me with confidence for the other half. Also to Stacy, who finds my drawings as funny as I do, and is as excited as I am that the book got finished.

To everyone who has ever told me I should be a writer, to everyone who encouraged and supported me, to everyone who dared to ask how the book was going, thank you. I love you and without all of you, this would have been a much harder task. Thank you.

To my Draft readers who helped me polish this diamond, thank you so much – your enthusiasm, your faith, your desire to read and your wonderful feedback helped make this book what she is.

To you dear reader. Thank you. This is for you. I hope you enjoy it and that it helps you to fall head over heels in love with your life.

CONTENTS

Introduction

Falling in love with life is something I've always wanted to do. For years, I wanted a "how to", a roadmap, a guide, a secret recipe. I could never find one, I just had to keep making little changes and hope that one day I'd figure it all out. In 2013 I did a survey of my lovely readers and clients, and one of the questions was "what stops you falling more in love with your life right now?" The top answer, with nearly 50% of respondents, was "I don't know how", so I know I am not alone in wondering 'how?'

What I have discovered is that it's a dance of a thousand steps; and you can do any of them or all of them, and of course there is no 'how' really – there's just a lot of little things you could do that will make you love life more and more and more.

Let me tell you now, **it is not an instantaneous process**. It takes time and effort from you (sorry) - but it is well worth it. Plus, all the suggestions in this book are fun. Falling in love with life isn't a boring, tedious process – it's one of fun and discovery and adventure and curiosity and happy dances.

Everyone is different, and what has worked for me may not work for you, but hopefully you will find enough ideas in here for you to start falling head over heels in love with your life, and you can add your own chapters – let me know what you add to your 'guide to falling in love with life'.

This moment is the only one you need to fall in love with. Ultimately, if you keep doing that over and over in every moment, you will fall head over heels in love with your life. This book will help you to have more and more moments that you love each day, because why wait to get happy?

By the way, there is nothing wrong with you if you do not currently love your life as it is. You are not defective. You are not failing. You are not a wailing mess with no hope of recovery. You're just human – we all have times when we're dancing through life, and others when we're wondering if this is it.

For most of us, we only need a few small changes to make a huge difference to how much we're enjoying our lives. So be inspired by this book to make small tweaks to your life so that you can have the best life possible for you today. Not next year or next decade or next lifetime. Now.

You can read this book from front to back or back to front or dip in to the headings that interest you. Try one idea from it a day, or one a week. Ignore 70% of it and fully embrace the other 30%. Try every single tip or try just a handful of things. In short, do what YOU want to do. Do what works for you. It's your life.

I will tell you this though, if you just read the book, you'll enjoy it (I hope). It won't help you fall in love with your life much if you don't DO anything with that knowledge. Take the tips and apply them, enjoy it, and tell me about it. Tell me what gets in the way of you falling in love with your life. Tell me what ideas you have tried and didn't like, or what ideas you tried and loved. Tell me how you fall in love with life.

Get in touch at donnaonthebeach.com.

Objections to loving life

After 10+ years of coaching, I've heard a LOT of objections about ideas that help you fall in love with life. I've made quite a few of the objections myself. So if you're reading this thinking 'yeah, but in the real world life isn't that Pollyanna-esque', or you think I'm overly optimistic or naïve, or using clichés or pointing out the bleeding obvious…

Well, you might be right on all counts, but entertain the possibility that I am also right. Just because someone is optimistic, it doesn't make them wrong. I used to be the negative, cynical, worldly person who thought the world was out to get me, and life pretty much sucked until you died.

I got over it.

I changed, I started to fall in love with life. You can too. Don't let your cynicism and pessimism get in your way.

If some of the chapters are just too hard to swallow for you right now, that's fine. Just ignore them. As long as some of them are hitting the spot for you, keep on reading. (If every chapter is irritating you, please stop reading and go do something else.) Some of these things will trigger you, will make you cross, will make you want to argue with me that 'life's just not like that'.

I know, 15 years ago, I'd have wanted to argue with me too. Instead of arguing, notice what's triggering you, what's getting up your nose, what's winding you up? If I assert that Aston Villa Football club are the best sports team in the world, you may disagree with me, but you probably won't get angry or irritated. So if you are reacting that way, it's a sign that there's something there to investigate and dig deeper into.

Also, some of the chapters won't be relevant to you (note: spoiler alert) – you may hate dancing or laughing or nature. If so, move on to the next chapter – this is not an instruction manual for life, it's a buffet. You can take the mini pizzas and leave the fish sticks. I have no desire to take over the world with clones of my ideas to enjoy life. For a start, you'd all be cluttering up my favourite places.

You may think 'it's easy for you to say'. Yes, it is easy to say – it's not always easy to live it, I know that. Many of the ideas in this book take a lot of effort and practice. You probably won't read them and change your entire outlook overnight. You may need reminding over and over again (I did. I still do).

You have a choice every moment of every day to choose to feel better and love life more, or not. Sometimes it is just easier to not feel better. As odd as that sounds, sometimes it is easier to do nothing than to make an effort to change things. I understand that, and I'm not saying "do all this in 5 minutes flat and change your life".

I'm saying some of these ideas can change your life if you put them into practice. It's not always as easy as 'do that, don't do that' – if it was, everyone's life would be perfect. Nevertheless, it is worth the effort to try making some changes and doing what's in your power to make your life better.

In the spirit of full disclosure, I am not a happy-clappy, always laughing, always dancing girl. I'm still on the journey to falling head over heels in love with life too. I'm with you on this path. I wrote this book as much to remind myself what I already know as to teach other people. Some days, I am a grouch. Some days, I don't like my life at all. Some of the circumstances of my life aren't perfect.

That's kind of my point. You don't have to be perfect. Your life doesn't have to be perfect. Fall in love with the life you have, whether it's good, bad or indifferent - and as it gets better you'll enjoy it even more (or as you enjoy it more, it gets better – that's just as true). It's a process, not an either/or. I love my life a thousand times more than I did 15 years ago, and I expect to keep loving it more and more and more.

I'm not sure anyone is 100% happy 100% of the time. In fact, a couple of the most joyous people I know recently shared that they had bad days, but they took control and turned the frown upside down.

Life can hit you right between the eyes with challenges at any point (and hormones can turn your world inside out at any point). What counts most is how you deal with it, and that's something we can learn. Together. Not from a 'hey, check me out, I'm perfect' place, but from a 'hey, this is what I know so far' place.

The craziest objection to loving life

One of the looniest objections I come across is the idea that it is somehow *selfish* to love your life. Seriously? The people who will be most affected by your happiness are your friends and family. They will get happy dust sprinkled all over them, like it or not. They will get the joy that comes with being with a joyful person. They will see what it looks like to love life.

They might even try it themselves. Instead of following a pattern of working too hard and taking zero care of themselves, they might follow a pattern of loving their life. Instead of seeing you hurting, angry and miserable, and having that hurt them (because it does hurt when a loved one isn't loving life), they will see you laughing and dancing and being joyous.

If you think your family and friends would prefer you being a bear with a sore behind, then stop reading now. However, I suspect they'd love it if you danced through life with a big smile on your face.

Part 1:

The Joy of

Being Alive

Revel in the joy of simply being alive

"I like living. I have sometimes been wildly, despairingly, acutely miserable, racked with sorrow, but through it all I still know quite certainly that just to be alive is a grand thing." - Agatha Christie.

I know sometimes that joy in being alive feels a million miles away and life utterly sucks, but you're alive. And while you're alive, there is possibility, opportunity, wonder and joy to be found. Many of us only get this feeling when we survive a near-death experience, or someone close to us dies and we fully understand, momentarily, what a gift it is to be alive.

When you're alive, things can change. While you're still breathing, joys can be found. Life itself is a truly wondrous thing – one we don't even fully understand yet. If you've witnessed (or given) birth, you may have felt that miracle of life feeling. You may have recognised that new life is miraculous (it's why people get gooey over puppies and babies and kittens).

Your life may have felt like a trial, it might have been horrible so far, but it is still a miracle that you are here, breathing, living, and alive. So find (if you can) the joy in that truth. Don't wait for near-death experiences or loss or shock health diagnoses to realise that to be alive is a magnificent thing.

When we're in the middle of being terribly busy and important and running endlessly on that hamster wheel, it doesn't always seem like a magnificent thing to be alive. It's a grind, a bore, an endless treadmill of 'same shit, different day', but truly, life is more than that when you stop to think about it.

Sometimes the circumstances of our lives cause us to forget the wonder, the joy, and the absolute marvel of life. We don't know what tomorrow will bring, what joys and sadness we'll experience, but we're here and we can experience them – fully, deeply, because we're here, we have a life to enjoy. So enjoy that very fact – it's a gift.

**"Find ecstasy in life; the mere sense of living is joy enough."
— Emily Dickinson**

See the wonder in the world

"When it's over I want to say, I was the bride married to amazement. I was the bridegroom taking the whole world in my arms." Mary Oliver

There's beauty all around. Can you see it? Yeah, on a drizzly grey cold miserable day it's tough to see the wonder in anything, but look anyway. Make the effort to see the magical, the wondrous, the beauty around you. It's in people, in animals, in the natural world, even in the man-made world.

Stop and smell the flowers, appreciate the architecture, savour the taste, enjoy the sunset, hear the birds sing, watch people laugh. Look for things to enjoy the beauty of - see the world through fresh, young, eager eyes (even if you feel stale, old and jaded). In fact, that's why we get stale, old and jaded because we stop seeing the wonder in life.

A child sees easily the wonder in the world - the beauty, the joy, the fun. Take lessons from the kids in your life about how to see the wondrous in the mundane. What fascinated you as a child? What would fascinate you now if you took the time to stop and look?

Clouds in the sky? Waves crashing on the shore? Stars? Sunsets? Beautiful writing? Amazing apps? Historical discovery? With the wonders of t'internet, we can share in most experiences, wherever we live. We can watch the waves crashing on 100 shores without leaving our couch; we can discover new worlds, new people, and new ideas without putting on a coat.

Truly, it's wondrous. Don't be blasé and jaded, get back in touch with your inner child and be fascinated by the fact that you can see someone as you speak to them from 1000 miles away (I remember when this was an impossible dream). Or if that doesn't inspire awe and wonder, find what does for you.

Life is full of fascinating people and places and animals and technologies and achievements and wonders of all stripes. When was the last time you allowed yourself to be impressed by something in the world? Whether it's how a spider spins their web, or how tomatoes grow from a teeny tiny seed, or how electricity powers everything from a toothbrush to a computer.

Take the time to notice all of the wondrous, beautiful, incredible things that surround you in your life – things that you normally take entirely for granted. There is so much to be enjoyed and admired and fascinated by. Put on your sparkly, wonder-full glasses and see it all.

Embrace what you love (even if it's deeply uncool)

What do you love to do? More importantly, what do you love to do that you're a little bit embarrassed about? Maybe the thing you only do when no one is watching. Like watching archaeological programs or reading kid's books or listening to classical music or knitting or dancing around to teen-pop boy band music (if you're not 12 anymore).

If you love opera, and sunsets, and afternoon tea, and dancing 'til dawn, and DVD days, and walks in the park, and crosswords, and Shakespeare, and reading trashy novels, and dancing around your kitchen, and singing into your hairbrush, own it. Embrace it - it's what you love. Even if embracing it means putting up with a raised eyebrow from your partner, or a mocking comment from a friend, own it. "Yes, I know it's nerdy...and I love it." (Maybe they just need permission to be deeply uncool too.)

It's not important to be cool. It's important to love *your* life. Not the life you think you should love. Not the life the magazines tell you is perfect. The life that is made up of the things that genuinely enthral you. The life that makes you giggle with sheer joy.

Don't try to be cool or only like the things your friends like. Instead, find, acknowledge and accept the things that you really like. Whatever brings you joy is cool, whatever you love is right for you - who cares who else joins in? Most often, you will find friends who will join you in your joys.

An old friend I once went clubbing with is my "Shakespeare-play-attending friend" - if you'd told me 15 years ago that we'd regularly be seen in Stratford taking in some thespian-shaped entertainment I'd have assumed you were on drugs. Since we started going, other friends who've never expressed one small interest in the theatre have suddenly decided they might like to go too.

Don't wait for anyone's permission to enjoy what YOU love - enjoy it anyway. Friends will join you. Or not. Who cares? If you love it, that's all that matters, own it and be ok with being uncool, geeky and off-trend. Trust me it's way more fun than standing in a *trendy* club you think is dreadful in *trendy* clothes you feel stupid in with *trendy* people who are boring you to death.

I know the cool kids teased you at school, and we all wanted to be in the most popular groups, but it's time to let that nonsense go. People mock because they don't understand. I once mocked someone for owning the Star Wars box set. I now own that box set. I just didn't realise how good it was. Let them not understand, and enjoy what you enjoy with or without their blessing.

You don't need anyone else's approval to enjoy Star Wars, or sunsets, or Shakespeare, or cheesy 80's music, or kids fiction, or terrible teen films, or cartoons, or anything else that's not trendy and popular and terribly stylish. If you feel you do need someone's permission, here is it:

You are hereby granted permission to like what you like, love what you love and enjoy what you enjoy, even (especially) if it's not *cool*.

I'm not 14 anymore, and I don't want to hang out with the popular people. Unless I like them, of course. It's not about what's cool, or trendy, or fashionable, or sick (hmm). It's about what's fun, what's energising, what makes me smile and dance and laugh and lose myself completely. For me, cool now has a new meaning. Cool isn't popular and fashionable, it's individual and unique; it's an energy of joy and love and lightness. Cool is enjoyment.

You'll never fall in love with your life if you're waiting for someone else to approve your joys, or if you're trying to enjoy things you don't really like in order to be down with the kids. Whatever gives you joy, that's what's right for you. Own it, enjoy it, embrace it, and fall in love with your unique loves.

As my friend Deb said "I would add it's never too late to become uncool. Whether you're 6 or 106, today's a gift. Be unabashedly joyful about your dorky loves — theatre, romantic novels, corny movies or knitting all of the scarves worn by the 4th Doctor (my daughter is on scarf #2). Tomorrow isn't guaranteed, so seize the day."

Don't forget, there are uncool things that your friends and family do that you just don't get either. Like camping. I don't get it. I mean, camping? In a tent? What's that all about? My opinion doesn't stop other people doing it, and nor should it. As long as they don't want me to sleep in a tent, what they get up to is totally their business. And what you get up to that's wonderfully nerdy is your business, so own it.

A list of joys

So, now you're owning your joys, it's time to get clear on exactly what does give you joy. Make a list of all the things that give you joy and do something off that list every day. Many of us never stop to think about what we enjoy, what we love, what gives us joy. We never re-evaluate as we grow older and change, we just moodle through life without really paying attention to our greatest joys.

So making a list can be a bit of an eye-opener. Sometimes you will sit with a blank expression on your face, not able to think of anything that gives you joy. Sometimes your list will contain one item. Sometimes you'll think of dozens of things, and you will probably discover that some of the things you thought gave you joy don't really.

This is surprisingly common - you either think a certain activity *should* give you joy or you know someone who gets lots of joy from that thing, so you try it yourself. But it doesn't bring you anything but frustration or boredom. Whenever you find anything like that, cross it off your list immediately. Make more room in your day for the things that truly bring you joy. Always remember, it's your life – it's what brings YOU joy.

This list is an ongoing, evolving, changing activity. What's on my list now is not what was on it 15 years ago, or 30 years ago (not that I had a joy list then. When I was a kid, I just knew what gave me joy). The joy list evolves as you evolve. 15 years ago going out drinking and clubbing with friends was high up the list – we did it every weekend, at least once.

Now, I don't drink and I haven't been clubbing for…hmm…it's probably been years, I can't even remember the last time I went to a club. What gave me joy in my 20's doesn't now I'm in my 40's. You may be different – I have friends who go clubbing more now than they did 20 years ago. Once again, it's your life my darling – the list is of *your* joys.

Some things will stay the same. Since I was old enough to do so I have loved to read and to daydream and to write and to watch animated kids films and to listen to music and sing into a hairbrush. Some things you'll have added as you go through life – for me, watching the stars, sitting on the beach watching the waves, and watching the sunset have all been added to my list.

If you are a bit flummoxed about what gives you joy, don't worry – if you've never thought about it before, it can be a perplexing question. Start with what you loved as a kid; add what you loved as a teenager; and on through the decades to now. Add things you think might give you joy if you gave them a try. Ask friends for ideas. Yes, it's your life, but sometimes a little inspiration can help – either to help you find your joys, or find what definitely isn't for you.

A client I shared this exercise with asked me for my list – which includes lots of solitary pursuits. I'm an introvert, so I get my energy from being alone. So there was yoga and meditation, and reading, and nature - all of which were like kryptonite to my client. As an extrovert, these solitary pursuits were not for them, so they then understood that their joys involved other people.

If the word 'joys' doesn't really work for you, try your 'favourite things' or 'things you love to do' list instead. It's the same difference, but sometimes the word 'joy' feels a bit grandiose, like it has to be a list of the most amazing things *evaahh*.

Things that give us joy can be small or silly – 30 seconds of silence before the day begins, a cupcake, stationery, rainbows. Joy lives in moments – some of them are big and memorable and amazing (wedding days, births of babies etc.); others are small and insignificant and also joyous.

Once you have your list, start doing things off that list regularly – every day if you can manage it. Now before you start waffling on about how you don't have time, you don't have to spend 800 hours a day doing the things that bring you joy. You can make the small things that give you joy part of your daily routine.

For example, taking 10 seconds to inhale the smell of your morning coffee, or popping outside for 2 minutes to look at the stars in the evening, or putting your favourite music on and car dancing all the way to work. (Responsibly, of course, you don't want to mosh into other cars.)

Don't make it a big chore. Just find a little pocket of time and do something from your joy list every day. (The added benefit of the joy list is that when you're feeling pecky/irritated/fed up, you have some foolproof cheer-me-ups.) You may start with 2 minutes of joyful moments, but as you keep making and finding time for your joys they will fill your life. Who wouldn't fall in love with a life full of things that bring them joy?

Shake your booty

Dancing is one of the best ways I know to feel better. It's enormous fun, great for raising energy, and a good way to shake off any negative energy. Dance it out. Whatever it is. Dance your joys, dance your sorrows, dance your lethargy, dance your energy. Dance it all out.

You do not have to put together a complicated modern dance routine that has you flinging yourself at walls. Nor do you need to learn the foxtrot, or ballet, or street dance. Simply put on some music, get up and move your body with the music. Your body will move in the way it wants to.

Some days it's enough to shuffle around slowly; some days you will be bouncing about the place; some days you will just want to stretch; some days you will pull out cheesy dance moves from your childhood, some days you will move in ways never seen on a dancefloor.

Whatever works for you. If you think you can't dance, or you hate to dance, dance anyway. Most people who don't like dancing just don't like dancing in public. I'm not asking you to dance in the street (although, if you fancy it, do it). Just put on a playlist at home, shuffle it and dance for a song or two. No one's watching, no one can see if you look like a dipstick. You don't have to do any steps, you can just sway, or shake your bottom.

I remember once making my cousin dance. He couldn't dance and never danced. I dragged him up onto the dance floor and made him do it anyway – I was the only one there who knew him, and guess what? He danced, and he enjoyed it. He was just self-conscious. You get over that by dancing.

I want you to know that I am not a Dancer. I am not classically trained. I have done all my dancing in clubs, kitchens and my office (all offices should have room for a dance floor) and my experience shows there's no problem that can't be made better by a good bop. I have solved:
- Writer's block
- Not knowing what to do next
- Migraine
- Brain overload
- No energy
- Feeling stiff and tense
- Being pissed off
- Feeling sad
- Feeling cold

All solved just by having a dance. Trust me, try it. You don't have to dance well, or publicly, or for hours. A song or two will do, ten minutes of movement. Just shake your booty and dance off whatever needs dancing off.

When's your playtime?

How much of your time is playtime? Do you play and have fun every day, or do you play once or twice a year, on holiday and at Christmas? Joyful lives need play, they need fun, they need you to enjoy your life. How can you fall in love with a life that only has work and chores and rest? Even if you love your work and chores and rest, it's not enough, you need playtime.

What can you do to play? How did you love to play as a child? Why not try those things again now? I loved Lego, so I got some. I loved bubbles, so I got a bubble gun. I loved colouring and drawing (even though my level of competence is stick people) so I got pens and paper to draw and colour with.

You may have enjoyed making mud pies, playing on the swings, climbing trees, playing cards, riding your bike, skipping, making snow angels, jumping in puddles, kicking through leaves, hitting/kicking/throwing a ball, running for no apparent reason, hide and seek, playing board games, splotching paint onto paper. None of these are things an adult can't do (I've done everything except the mud pie in the last 2 years. I never liked mud pies.)

You may find they're not so much fun now, but try anyway, find what you love in your playtime. Experiment with new ideas, don't just have obsessive playing of Candy Crush as your only playtime. These days much play involves daft computer games that are not so much fun as compulsive. That's not the playtime I'm talking about.

I'm talking about doing things that you love, just for fun. Not for some specific end, not for gain, not to get gold stars, but just because you want to play. If you need a reason to play (other than because you can), play is good for you. It is healthy to play and have fun. It gives your brain a rest from being focused, your body a rest from being tense, your heart a rest from being serious and your spirit a boost.

Play deprivation can lead to depression. Most of the clients I have worked with over the years who have been down when we start have forgotten to play. Sometimes we forget even how to play. Because we're too busy being mature and sensible and dealing with the problems of life.

Here's the trouble: maturity is way over-rated. Sensible has its place, but it's not that much fun. Problems need play too. The deeper you go into the problems in your life, the harder it is to solve them. When you play, you free yourself up for all sorts of creative solutions; or the problem just fades into the background for even just a short time while you're playing.

I get that sensible people in your life may pull a face at the foolish, childish, inane nature of play, but you don't have to tell them. Although you could get them to read this chapter because they probably need playtime even more than you do. Play helps you to relax, lighten up, de-stress, feel good, have fun, and love your life.

So take some time to play – as often as you can. It's not enough to say 'I'll play when X, Y and Z are done' because you probably won't. Until you make play important and realise how necessary it is for you, you'll just put it off. Take the time, book it in your diary, and look for opportunities to make playtime part of your daily routine.

Get your silly on

When we're kids we can't wait to grow up and be mature and do adulty things. Then we grow up and get mature and are adulty, and we forget how to be silly. I mean, dahling, I have a reputation to uphold, I need to be sensible and rational and serious, people need to see that I am grown up and in control and responsible.

Well, I blow a raspberry in the general direction of that idea. Despite what you might have picked up from adults telling you not to be silly in your youth, there's nothing wrong with being silly and frivolous. In fact, silly is essential for the full enjoyment of life.

"An enlightened person is a continuous laughter.
He is not a serious man, as ordinarily thought.
Whenever you see seriousness,
Know well something is wrong—
Because seriousness is part of a diseased being.
No flower is serious unless it is ill.
No bird is serious unless it is ill.
An awakened man realises life is a song."
                    - Osho

Whose idea was it that as you got older, you have to grow up, behave maturely and get serious? What idiot came up with that one? I guarantee you that I will not meet my maker wishing I had taken myself more seriously, but I suspect I will wonder why I didn't laugh more, be silly more, entertain myself more, dance more, fart around more, play more.

Kids know how to do this instinctively before they become self-conscious. They know how to play and draw and bounce and run around and jump and giggle and pull faces and be silly. We knew once too. If we can rediscover our inner silly, playful, fun, creative, laughing, joyful child, we can stick our tongue out to those who think adults should be sensible and serious and boring and just have some fun and enjoy life.

One of my favourite quotes of all time is this:

"We are here on Earth to fart around. Don't let anybody tell you any different." Kurt Vonnegut

Farting around is defined in the Free Dictionary as 'fooling around', 'frittering time away'. It's one of my favourite pastimes. I love to moodle, to potter, to play, to mess around, to just do what I feel like doing at any particular time.

Most of the time, most of us don't have time to fart around, we're far too busy being sensible, serious, working, responsible, rational, earnest human beings, working and making our way in the world. There's work to be done, and chores to be done, and self-improvement to be done, and duties to be taken care of, and responsibilities to shoulder.

Well, why not try putting down those weighty issues and get into some constructive farting around. I am not suggesting that you abandon your duties and responsibilities, or jack in your job, but that you pay some attention to enjoying yourself, fooling around and kick up your heels a bit. Be silly, be frivolous, take off the serious shackles and enjoy the ridiculousness in life.

Sing

I have always loved to sing. Not in public, not for fame and fortune (fortunately because my voice is not meant for public consumption), just to sing along to my favourite tunes. I realised early in life the power of music – that singing along to songs that seemed to understand how I felt was cathartic, fun and surprisingly healing.

I have favourite songs that I sing to when I'm sad, when I have PMT, when I need cheering up, when I wish to express my joy in living. That's the power of song – it can help you express how you feel and it can cheer you up and make you feel better. Who cares if you sound good – get your hairbrush and belt out an old favourite.

The other thing about singing is (and you'll have to forgive me for being a bit woo-woo here) that it's a way for you to have a voice. A way for your voice to be heard. (If only by yourself and the dog. Who joins in by barking at you, which is clearly appreciation, right?)

So many of us go through life not letting our voice be heard, not letting our truth escape, not saying what we want to say. Singing allows us a voice, it allows us to say 'I'm not ok', or 'I have a dream' or 'supercalifragilisticexpialidocious'. (Lol – autocorrect has not tried to change my spelling of that.)

Sometimes you need to say it. Not so that someone in particular can hear you, just so that you've said it, or sung it. Now, just in case you're not sure about this tip – it's scientifically proven that singing decreases stress hormones, strengthens the immune system, and stimulates the pleasure centre of the brain. Honestly. Check on Auntie Google if you don't believe me.

Know what makes your soul sing and do it

One of the things that makes my soul sing is to write. I love to write. I love to share the millions of crazy thoughts that fly through my brain on a daily basis. For years, I clipped the wings of this particular eagle. I would only let myself do this activity that made my soul sing so much if it was work-related.

Hmm. Not so soul-singy. A bit more soul-muttery, frankly. Here's what I don't get: if it makes your soul sing, why wouldn't you do it? I never had an adequate answer to that question, and I suspect you don't either. We have to contend with all this stupid conditioning about being an adult and responsibility and having good reasons to do things.

Here's a reason: it makes my soul sing.

Do I need another reason? Do I need to make money from it? Do I need it to be good? Do I need it to have a purpose? Or could the fact that it makes my soul sing be enough? Could I just do it because I love to do it? Does it make any sense to you to put off doing things that make your soul sing? (If it does, please tell me, because I really don't get it, and I do it.)

Anyway, one minor obstacle to doing what makes our soul sing is that we don't know what makes our soul sing. We get put into a box and we forget that we even have a soul, never mind that it has a song. Well, take this as your reminder that you do have a soul and that it sings. Now, you get to enjoy the delicious exploration phase to find out what makes your soul sing.

You probably have a few ideas already – go and try them out. Some of the other things that make my soul sing are: sunsets, sunrises (it's me not being a morning person that gets in the way of this one), music, dancing, singing, drawing daft and random stick drawings, reading, theatre, live music and cinema, learning, rainbows, sunshine, walking in nature.

Any of them appeal? Try them. Notice if your soul sings or shrugs. If these things make your soul say 'meh', move on and find the things that your soul adores and do them. Not for a living, not to achieve a goal, not because you think you should or because someone else's soul sings because of it. Do it just because your soul sings when you dance around your room singing into a hairbrush. Or whatever works for you.

Make your top focus ENJOYING life

What would you say your top focus is in life right now? Your work? Your family? Making money? Surviving? How about enjoying life? Where does that come in on the list? Oh, I know, it's not like you're a student anymore. You're a big grown up with big girl shoes and you're mature and responsible and you have Very Important Duties to perform.

But seriously, where does enjoying life come on your list of priorities? 8th? 25th? Not on the list at all? One of the things I struggled with when I became an adult was how sensible you were supposed to be (and to be honest, I never really felt like an adult 'til I was 40, and even now I have moments of 'what? *I'm* a grown up? NO!'), and then I realised why I struggle with it so much.

It's a stupid rule. Who said adults had to get boring and stop laughing and never have any fun (unless it was adult, mature approved fun)? Who said frivolous was bad? Who said silly was not something good? Who made these rules of adulthood? I am making up a new rule of adulthood:

Rule of adulthood #1: Enjoy Life!

Yeah, maybe you do need to prioritise family and work and making money so you don't end up destitute under a bridge. Also, you want to make the most of your life. You want to enjoy your life. Your family and friends love it when you are enjoying life. You're a nicer colleague when you're enjoying life.

And, well, not to put too fine a point on it, isn't that the whole point of life? To enjoy it? Not to put your nose firmly on the grindstone until you die?

To begin to make enjoying your life a priority, you'll need to figure out what that means to you. We've talked already about creating a list of things that give you joy and owning your joys, so that's a good start. Now you get to explore it even further. What would make you enjoy life a little more today? Right now? It might be something from your joy list, it might be kicking something off your to-do list.

Furthermore, if you haven't redefined what enjoying life means to you since you were a student, you may want to look at it again. To me, when I was a student, enjoying life was being out with friends partying A LOT. There was a lot of clubbing and dancing and vodka and black Russians and pizza at 3 am and getting in at 7 am. If I tried to live that life now, I would not enjoy it.

For a start, I don't drink. Also, I am not a fan of clubs anymore (see not drinking). Lastly, although I don't mind an all-nighter or a late night now and again, mostly I like to wake up before lunchtime and see daylight. Enjoying life for me now means a nice mix of friend time and alone time, it means lots of books and writing and learning and creating. It means work that challenges me and inspires me. It means having the freedom to follow my inspiration.

The only things that stayed the same are dancing and friends. Everything else that means an enjoyable life for me has changed. What does an enjoyable life mean now to you?

Try this exercise with me: put your hand over your heart, take 3 deep breaths into your heart, and ask your heart "How much am I enjoying life right now on a scale of 1-10, where 1 is 'I'm not' and 10 is 'I LOVE MY LIFE'?" Let your heart answer – your head will try to butt in and argue it should be higher or lower, but let your heart answer.

Whether your number is a 2 or an 8, your mission is to move it up one. From 2 to 3; from 5 to 6; from 8 to 9. You can again ask your heart what you could do today to move it up just one point. Don't make it complicated and try to change your entire life overnight. Let it be simple and start to make enjoying your life *more* of a priority than it currently is.

Enjoy kids' stuff

I am an 8-year-old in a 40-ahem year old's body. I love kid-lit, I love animated movies. (Despicable Me? LOVE it.) I also like games, just like I did when I was 8 years old. I didn't grow out of it, I'm still a big kid at heart. If I'm feeling a little blue, one of my favourite things to do is curl up with a Harry Potter book or The Faraway Tree, or watch The Jungle Book.

If you have kids and you've had to watch The Little Mermaid 600 times, you may be over the kids' stuff. What about the kids' stuff you loved as a child? Pull one of those out of the bag - not for your kids but for your inner child. If you don't have kids, and you have no excuse to watch Aladdin, or The Sword in the Stone, watch them anyway.

Until I read Gretchen Ruben's 'The Happiness Project', I never knew that 'kid lit' was a thing. I didn't realise that adults could be into a genre of writing that is primarily aimed at kids. I thought it was just me. The Mr Men, Harry Potter, the Faraway Tree, Anne of Green Gables. I love them all.

What books, films and games did you love as a kid? What books, films and games have you not watched/read/tried because you're too grown up? Get over this *being an adult* nonsense, and have some fun. Not for intellectual stimulation, not so you'll look well-read and impress your book/film-snob mates, not for any reason but to feed your inner child.

We all have an inner child who is too often ignored, abandoned and dismissed when we get to be a mature, sensible adult. Your inner child deserves better. Plus, she's the gatekeeper of your joy. She's the part of you that CAN fall head over heels in love with life.

The adult part of you is probably still concerned about her dignity, her reputation, her responsibilities or some such nonsense, but the child in you can be wildly enthusiastic about this wonderful adventure of life. An adventure where panthers talk, spells work and mops and buckets dance. Feed your inner child with some kid stuff, and let me know what you're reading/watching/playing – if I haven't read/seen/played, I'll give it a go. :-D

Lose yourself in the moment

Where do you lose yourself? At the pictures (movies)? At the theatre? During a gig? Singing or playing music? Reading a book? While you're dancing? Doing yoga? Watching the sunset? Writing? Knitting? Painting? Loving time with your sweetheart? Also, when was the last time you let yourself get lost in something you enjoy?

Adults sometimes forget how to lose themselves in things. They forget to be mesmerised by something or someone because they've got a to-do list it would take a hundred years to complete and four thousand things to remember. Who can lose themselves when there's all that going on?

The good news is – you can. If you give yourself the chance to. We all lose ourselves in something – whether it's just the mundane tasks of driving or cleaning, or in something we love. You have to give yourself the opportunity to do it. Allow yourself to lose yourself in things that really move you.

I cannot lose myself in a book that's boring. Give me a good book though, and it'll be 4 o'clock in the morning before I know it. I can't lose myself in a gym session – I'm too busy checking the clock to see when I can leave. However, if you give me some music and let me dance without a clock to check, or put me at a gig of a band I love, I won't notice a damn thing happening around me for a couple of hours.

If you're in charge of little people, you cannot always totally lose yourself in the moment, because you'll look up and your child will be wandering off, causing mayhem, or sat with another family happily eating their picnic (happened to a friend of mine – she was frantic, her child was covered in jam and the other family were in fits of laughter). However, you can lose yourself in the moment *with* them – in stories and building bricks and mud pies and laughing for no reason.

Or you can find ways to lose yourself in just a short moment while someone else is in control of the small people. Everyone has reasons they can't lose themselves in something – usually because we're all far too busy and important. This is important too – it's giving yourself the gift of time to lose yourself in the moment.

It doesn't have to take hours either. Stopping to listen to a really great song can take 3-4 minutes. A friend of mine loses herself in the ironing – she goes onto auto-pilot while her mind wanders off to more exciting places.

That place of being lost in something or someone is a joyful, wondrous place. If it's a place you don't visit very often, that's a shame. Because going to that place often, going to that state of being will help you fall head over heels in love with your life. So, let yourself be lost in the things you enjoy.

Laugh easily and often (and for no reason)

Do you remember when you were a kid and you would start laughing with your friends; then someone would say 'what are you laughing at?' and the laughter would redouble because you didn't know what you were laughing at, you were just laughing. For no good reason. This makes the puzzled person standing opposite you asking what you're laughing at incredibly funny.

I love a good laugh. Laughing is one of my favourite things. Laughing for no reason is one of my favourite, favourite things. I can still remember occasions when I laughed and laughed and laughed with friends and we had no idea why we were laughing. (On one memorable occasion it took days to apologise to the friend who thought we were laughing at her – we weren't, it was just so funny that we didn't know why we were laughing that we couldn't tell her for laughing.)

Laughter is also very good for you (I don't think you hear enough about the health benefits of laughter). It lowers stress, boosts immunity, gives your tummy and lungs a good workout, triggers the release of endorphins, it's fun and you feel good. What's not to like about it?

Unfortunately, when we become mature, sensible, adults, we stop laughing. Children laugh easily and often (and for no good reason). Adults laugh less in comparison. Which is sad. There's nothing better than a good laugh, so why would you stop doing it?

I know it's not a deliberate thing for most of us – we don't wake up one day without a sense of humour. We just become a bit bogged down by life and forget to laugh, or we believe the adults that tell us that being a giggler is a bad thing. Ok, I accept it's not appropriate to chortle and snicker all day long or in certain circumstances; but mostly, laughter is to be welcomed, not shut off.

"A day without laughter is a day wasted." - Charlie Chaplin.

I couldn't agree more. Don't waste a day of your life – laugh easily, often and for no good reason. A couple of years ago I did a daily practice of laughing for a month and dedicated myself to the practice of laughing every day. Deliberately and purposefully.

I sought out things that made me laugh. I tried laughter yoga (brilliant), I looked up silly jokes and comedians I like. I looked for quotes on laughter. I made it my mission in life to laugh. That month was fun and light, and easy. My days were easier, my work went more smoothly, I was less grumpy, and I felt better. Just because I spent 10 minutes or so a day seeking to laugh.

It's that easy. Don't wait for the comical to come and find you – go looking for it. Share your favourite jokes (send them to me, I love jokes) and your favourite silly YouTube clips (YouTube is comedy gold), look up your favourite comedians and comedy shows, spend more time with people who make you laugh. Put laughter at the top of your to-do list.

Part 2:

Inner Wisdom

Learn to switch off

We live in a world where we are assaulted daily with an astonishing amount of information. It's hard to fall in love with your life when your brain is busy frying. So when was the last time you took some quiet time? Your mind will thank you for taking the time to meditate, to walk in nature, or just to sit and ponder with no distractions.

Your brain needs rest, it needs to switch off and recuperate. It needs to do something mindless. Surfing the net and watching TV are not as mindless as you might think. Anything that adds more information (even if that information is what some reality fool did last week) is not that relaxing for the brain.

As one of my clients beautifully put it:

"We can't hear truth over noise."

Even just switching everything off and sitting watching the sky for a minute counts here. In fact, why not try that? It feels odd to begin with because we try to fill every spare minute with either doing or consuming information or both. Unfortunately, that leads to mind fog, stress, overwhelm and in extreme cases, bat-crap crazy meltdowns.

I'm sure you've experienced that – when your mind just feels so full that you cannot think. Mind needs space to relax, to rest, to refresh; and when you do this you give yourself a better chance to notice 'hey I'm not enjoying this' or 'hey, I love x'. Inspiration can't get into your mind when you're filling it with endless chatter.

You need space to cogitate and ponder and mull and play. Filling every moment with stuff to do is a recipe for exhaustion, misery and eventually, breakdown. Learn to switch off and take the space for your brain to file away what it needs to and throw away what it doesn't need.

The added and beautiful benefit of this is that when you stop, you can hear inner wisdom, inspiration and soul calls. When there's too much noise, you can't hear anything. Whenever I stop to meditate, or walk, or take a dance break, I always find an inspired idea or answer to a problem pops into my mind – give yourself the space to allow that to happen.

Trust yourself

It's your life - trust yourself to make good decisions regarding your life. Everyone and his dog has an opinion and has advice for you, but they are not you. It is not their life. I nearly went out of business within 2 years, because I trusted everyone else's opinion over my own.

I listened to all the respected and accepted wisdom about marketing and sales, but it just didn't work for me. I'm not a corporate drone, I don't talk about ducks in rows (unless I'm being sarcastic), and I find the corporate marketing painfully dull. I tried and tried to put my star shape into a square hole, to the point that I realised I couldn't do it and was ready to give up altogether.

Fortunately, at that point, I worked with a coach who helped me to find MY way to do business, and my business was saved - HALLELUJAH! I am not suggesting you dismiss all advice. Just trust yourself MORE than you trust someone else.

The marketing advice I was getting made my skin crawl a bit. It made me feel sick. It made me pull the ick face. At the time, I thought I just wasn't cut out for bizniz, but then I realised my inner wisdom was talking to me. It wasn't even subtle. Yours isn't either. If you are feeling there's something off about a situation, a person, or some advice, listen to that – listen to yourself.

Even if someone else has done exactly what you want to do, that doesn't mean that you have to do it their way. (Have you never heard Frank Sinatra's 'My Way'?) We're all individual, unique, a special blend of personality and characteristics and experiences. What works for me may not work for you. Mrs Xpert may have "The System That Works For Everyone", but it might not be for you. It's your life. You get to do it your way.

So trust in yourself. Trust in your inner wisdom. Back yourself 100%. Trust that even if friends, family or even society at large would disagree with you, it's YOUR life. You have to live it your way. You have to trust that your instincts are good. You have to stand up for what you know is right for you. You must honour yourself.

We all have an inner sense of what is right for us, and it doesn't matter how many people tell us we're wrong, we just *know*. Like I just *know* that a snooze in the afternoon is far more effective than sitting slumped at my desk with spaghetti for brains, no matter how many people think that snoozing in the day is lazy, bad, wrong, cheating or shows poor work ethic.

It's difficult to trust ourselves at first, because since we were kids we learned to fit in, to do the sensible, logical thing. When we come up with a plan we know someone else is going to disagree with, we want to win them over, convince them; but we're really trying to convince ourselves. When you just trust your inner knowing, you just do it. You share it, but you don't need to justify it to make someone else feel better about it, because you trust in yourself.

If you know that yoga/meditation/belly dancing are good for you, do them, no matter how many people think you're nuts or woo-woo. If you know (as I do) that you work better when you are rested and you get to work on fun stuff, do it; no matter how many people think you should work with your nose to the grindstone 24/7 and ne'er let a creative, joyful moment infect your work day. If you know it is right for you to have an unconventional life, live that life. The alternative is soul-destroying.

Of course, friends and family have an opinion. They are entitled to that opinion. You are entitled to ignore it. It's *your* life. It's *your* inner knowing. It's *your* connection to what's right for you. Without that connection, we feel lost and confused and we take all the conflicting advice available and wonder why it doesn't work for us. We were born as individuals. We need to live as individuals. Trying to be a Stepford Person is painful. Allow yourself to be who you really are. Trust your inner knowing. Stand up for your true self. Live YOUR life.

Learn to trust yourself - learn to hear your own inner wisdom, learn to understand your body, mind, heart and soul's signals, learn to hear your inner yes, and to trust it. It might not lead you to exactly where you thought you would go, but it won't lead you far wrong, and you might just go somewhere better than you expected.

Hear your heart's whispers

Your heart is always whispering to you. It sends you messages of love and joy and possibility and yearning, and the more you ignore it, the more it hurts. You cannot fall in love with your life if you ignore your heart completely.

Your heart wants to be heard. It wants you to know how loved you are, how much love you are capable of, how much you could love life if you listened to those heart whispers.

We've all felt and heard the wisdom in our hearts – we've felt the heart leap, we've felt the love, and we've also felt the hurt and the pain and the loss in our hearts. So sometimes we close down so we don't feel that hurt any more. That's what I did. It hurt to feel, so I stopped feeling.

Only I didn't really, I just locked the hurt in. Which was kind of dumb as I look back on it because I didn't want to lock it in, I wanted to let it go. Anyway, I also locked in my dreams and desires and wishes and hopes, and my loves and joys – all were locked in with the hurt.

Once I started to take down some of the walls around my heart, the wishes and hopes and desires and dreams were still there, and my heart was still whispering away. I had barely been able to hear those whispers because of the walls I'd put up.

There comes a point when ignoring your heart becomes too painful – it was then that I started to listen. Now, I check in with my heart every day. Every day I get a message from my heart – because it is always talking.

Your heart is always whispering messages of love and longing. Not in a moony-eyed romantic novel sort of way, but in an 'ooh, do this, try this, you are safe, you are loved' kind of way. In an 'I believe in you' way. In a 'you are worthy' way. In an 'I love you, even though you're a massive geek who loves spreadsheets' way (or maybe that's just my heart).

So try this: Take a deep breath. And another. And one more. Begin breathing into your heart, and ask yourself "what does my heart want me to know today?" Give your heart a chance to answer – give it time. (Not just 4 seconds like most of my clients do the first time I take them through this exercise.) It will probably be a simple answer, and it will be loving.

If you get a "what the hell do you think you're doing?" type message, trust me, that is not your heart. Your heart is unconditionally loving and supportive – even when you're being a psycho, PMT-crazed bitch from hell (or maybe that's just my heart).

Keep talking to your heart, start to get those hopes and dreams out in the open. You may not be ready to hear it all, but your heart knows you; it'll keep the biggest dreams and craziest wishes safe until you're ready to hear them. Talk to your heart every day. Get used to hearing the whispers of your heart, and of course, start to follow those whispers and making those wishes and hopes and dreams your reality.

Hear your soul's whispers

Just like your heart, your soul is also always whispering to you. Your soul will call you to be the very best, most joyful, most vibrantly alive that you can be. Your soul wants you to follow your dreams and enjoy your life. Your soul will not rest if you are in a soul-destroying situation. It is always whispering - are you listening?

It's that voice that calls to you "fly, fly, fly". It's the insistent voice that tells you that you CAN do it. It's the nagging feeling that there must be more to life. It's the part of you that won't let you settle for less than your best life. It's the part of you that's connected to the divine, the source, the energy of life. It's the part of you that *knows*.

For years, I could only barely hear a soul whisper that I thought was dissatisfaction. It was a whisper that said, "there is more to life". I had a good job and a good lifestyle and was heading down the path to the career, house, man, car, washing machine. Sadly I was bouncing off the walls of that life. I couldn't understand why until I started listening more to my inner wisdom than I did to how I'd expected life to turn out.

I expected a normal life – with a career working for someone else, and a husband and a house and some kids and a dog, but my soul kept saying "No" and creating this vague feeling of discontent until I started to listen and do things that made me feel alive.

For me, it was to have my own business, and ultimately to write this book. Did my soul pipe down then? Nope. She's still talking – the only difference is that now I trust her implicitly, and I can hear her clearly most of the time. She's the part of me that sees the potential of what I and my life could be, and she doesn't want me to settle for anything less than that.

She's the part of me that won't be satisfied with anything less than 100% in love with life, dancing with joyous abandon through a life that challenges and excites and scares me. She's the one that takes my hand and runs into the unknown with a breathless laugh. Perhaps you recognise her? Perhaps you've heard a soul just like her whispering 'fly, fly, fly'?

Try this: Take a deep breath. And another. And one more. Ask yourself "what does my soul want me to know today?" Give it more than a few seconds, it may take time to come through if you've never taken the time to listen to your soul before. *Top tip: Your soul doesn't think you suck. She may tell you some truths, but she'll never do it in a mean or demeaning way.*

Please don't panic that your soul will make you do utterly terrifying things. Your soul knows you from the inside – she knows what scares you, what you feel you're capable of, what holds you back. Not only will she give you the destination, but she'll also give you the guidance and baby steps to get there too. If my soul had told me even 2 years ago that I'd be writing a book and illustrating it too, I'd still be hiding under the bed.

Step by step, my soul has led me on and now, here I am, creating stick drawings, writing the first of many books (well, the third, but I'm re-writing the other two, so I consider this number one). Your soul's been whispering to you all the time – all you need to do now is to tune in and start listening to her. She has the answers you've always wanted.

Trust me, you want to hear what she has to say, and she wants you to hear her.

Make decisions on the toss of a coin

How do you make a decision? Do you weigh up the options carefully, plumping for the safest, cheapest, easiest, and most sensible? Do you worry endlessly about the consequences and never make a decision at all? Or do you jump in and make a decision and worry about the consequences later?

For many years I have tried (and failed) to do the first of these – and do the *right* thing. The problem is, the *right* thing is often the *wrong* thing for me. The sensible decision is usually the one decision which will stifle my spirit, bore me to tears or keep me in a situation I hate. I like flying by the seat of my pants – it's far easier than all this pros and cons bull. I now toss a coin to help me decide.

The simplicity of a coin toss appeals to me because it is quick, easy and relatively uncomplicated – no evidence gathering, no researching, no discussing, just a flip and there you have it – a decision. I don't just mean for small decisions, like pizza or pasta? I have decided whether to buy a house, go to Australia for a year, leave my job to start my own business, and buy a car - all on the toss of a coin.

I can see some of you twitching at the very idea of this – not exactly scientific, responsible or sensible, right? Correct. I'll tell you what it does do though, it focuses you very quickly on what YOU want. Imagine you wanted to decide whether to look for a new job, you toss a coin and it comes up tails - stay at your current job.

Your stomach sinks, you stare at the coin and think 'best of 3'. Then best of 5, best of 7, best of 9, best of 73. You see, I'm not suggesting you take the advice of the coin. That would be ridiculous. Although if you really don't care whether you have pizza or pasta, it helps you make the decision.

Merely flipping the coin will tell you what you really want – in the above example, you want to leave the job. The coin gets you in touch with your intuition, your inner wisdom, and your knowingness. Furthermore, it's quick. In 3 seconds, the coin is flipped and you're either happy or looking for 'best of 3'.

Of course, not all decisions will be that easy – sometimes you will then need to talk your mind round to the crazy decision your intuition has made for you, not to mention you have to try to explain to friends that you're not buying a house after all, you're buying a rucksack and going off to the other side of the world alone. (It freaks them out when you've never expressed the slightest interest in travelling or rucksacks before.)

Even though sometimes you will still have some internal to-ing and froing to do about your decision, this technique will help you cut to the chase most of the time. As well as saving you a lot of time in agonising over pros and cons. Time that could be better and more productively spent doing fun things.

Follow your inspiration

We all have inspired ideas all the time – usually those really random ideas you get at 2 am that make perfect sense in the middle of the night but wither in the cold light of day. They're the ones we often talk ourselves out of, with our logical, linear, sensible training. If you shrug off that training and start listening to those random thoughts; and then following them, you will enter a new and magical world.

I am not exaggerating. Inspiration is a beautiful thing. It's your soul talking to you. It's the Divine Spark. It's creative juice. It's fun. Everyone I know who follows their inspiration – whether that involves creating or travelling or cooking or arranging events or singing or whatever – enjoys life more than those who don't.

Not following inspiration makes the inspired voice go really quiet – sometimes so quiet that you can't hear it anymore. That is beyond saddening to me. Because that inspiration is a spark of joy that can light the fire of loving life. Your inspired ideas will take you somewhere. You may not know where, but they will take you somewhere. Often to places you never thought you would go.

What happens as a result of you following your inspiration is out of your sphere of influence – you can't make people buy your book or your program or support the business you were inspired to begin. Still, following your inspiration may bring unseen and often unsung benefits. Starting my blog was the beginning of a journey that helped me to become the writer I'd always wanted to be – I honed my craft, and in doing so, I've created a staggering body of work.

Those articles and blog posts are always there, ready to help whoever they're for (including me). That blog has brought me so much joy, it's challenged me, it's helped me to start to get over my fear of being seen in the world, it's helped me to get more comfortable championing my work, it's helped me meet people I'd never have met, it's led to some interesting collaborations, it's helped and inspired thousands of people over the last 8 years.

If I only judged the success of that inspired action by how much money the blog brought in, I would have missed the point by a country mile. And I probably would have stopped long before all the benefits and gifts became obvious.

Inspired action works that way – you don't know what amazing gifts it will bring you, but it will bring gifts. It's inspired. It's given to you by the Divine, whatever your definition of that is (God, inner self, the universe, muse). Do you trust the Divine? Do you trust that what you're inspired to create and do is given to you?

If so, why would you hesitate? Why would you throw the gift of inspiration back in the face of the Divine? Personally, I have hesitated out of fear, out of lack of confidence in me, I've thrown the gift back because I didn't understand inspiration, because I *didn't* trust the Divine, I've done it because frankly, it seemed too easy.

Inspired action is easy. It's fun. It's joyful. It's sometimes challenging, and your brain, heart and soul feel like they've been wrung out by the effort involved. Ultimately it feels right though, and you just find yourself doing it (even if your brain is arguing that you don't want to write this book or take this action, 10 minutes later, you are).

Inspiration works for you; and if you follow it, your life will become a delicious adventure of inspired action and joyful days. It may not bring the results you think you want, your return may not be what you expect, but it may just be even better. Trust the gift of the Divine/muse/inner self/universe and follow your inspiration, wherever it may lead.

Learn to hear and follow your inner yes

You have inside you a foolproof guidance system – an inner GPS if you will - that will help you to have the life you will most enjoy if you learn to hear it and follow it. The beauty of this system is that it has been active for your whole life. You may have heard it when you decided to jump ship from the job that sucked all the joy from your world. You may have heard it screaming 'NO' when you started dating that guy. You know the one. The one you *knew* you shouldn't go out with. Yep, him.

You may have spent many years tuning out this guidance system and living life according to a set of logical, sensible, thought-through decisions and a 5-year plan that left you feeling slightly empty inside, but with lots of ticks on the goals on your plan. It will still have been advising you. Perhaps you feel it as a vague dissatisfaction, perhaps you feel it as a flash of inspiration, perhaps you feel it in your tummy – either as butterflies or uncomfortable churning.

I could talk for hours about your inner guidance system. For now, I will just talk about your inner YES. (Plus inner NO, by extension.)

This is the feeling you get inside when you know that something is for you, and then you talk yourself out of it because it's barmy.

It was the feeling that told me to go backpacking to Australia (I couldn't have been a less likely candidate for backpacking), it was the feeling that told me to do a coaching course, to start a business, to write this book. I could easily have talked myself out of all of these ideas, but I didn't. I trust my inner yes. In 2014, I started living my life according to that inner yes.

As much as possible, I make the choice that's a YAY (not a NAY or an OKAY) – I make the choices that feel good to me. To do with my business, my relationships, my money, my health, my whole life. That's the great thing about the inner yes, it's always on. It's always ready to give guidance. All you need to do to tune in is to notice how you feel.

Try this now: think of something or someone you love and notice what happens in your body. You may get an involuntarily smile, your heart may expand, you may get a fizzy feeling in your heart or tummy, your throat may feel giggly. What does it feel like to you? Where do you feel it?

Now think of someone or something you don't like and notice what happens in your body. You may tense up, make an 'ugh' face involuntarily, your stomach may churn, your heart may sink, your throat might tighten, your muscles might tense. What does it feel like to you and where do you feel it?

That's your inner yes and no. Often your reactions will be very subtle, so the more you can practice, the better you will get at reading the signals of your body and emotions. So this week, why not practice before you make any decision – what to have for lunch, whether to meet friends or have a night in, what work to focus on – ask your inner guidance system to give you a yes or a no.

As much as you can, follow your inner yes. When you spend your days feeling tense and unhappy because they're full of things your inner NO is screaming about, that's hard to love. Life is so much more enjoyable when you are doing things you really want to do. Of course, you'll still have to do things you don't want to – dentists and such - but if your life generally consists of things your inner YES is approving, it'll be so much easier to fall in love with it.

Trust that life is happening for you, not to you

What if life was All Good, Always? What if the things that happen to you in life were FOR you, not proof that the Gods hate you? What if you believed in an unseen force of good at work in your life? That even when things seem to be going against you that there would be some kind of gift in the situation for you?

Some of you will be scowling at the page right now, I know. This attitude is often seen as naïve, unrealistic and foolish. Much more realistic is the cynicism and negativity that has people saying the world will end every 5 minutes. Well, forgive me for pointing out the bleeding obvious here, but the cynical, negative worldview is no more realistic than the positive, optimistic, universe loves me attitude.

Honest. Most of the dire predictions never come about. The sky has not fallen in, Chicken Little. World War Three (perhaps surprisingly, she said a little cynically) has not started yet. It still may, but to my knowledge, it has been confidently predicted for the last 30 years (I remember newscasters banging on about it in the '80s). More realistic, huh? Hmm.

The point here is that you tend to get what you expect in life. There are psychological, neurological and sciencey explanations for this, but the upshot is that if we see a job loss or a relationship ending as the worst thing ever, we will experience it that way. If we seek the silver linings, we find them. It's that simple. If you are expecting life to be good for you, it's a much happier place to be.

I know it's hard to see sometimes, and other times it's bloody impossible to see any silver lining in a loss – especially when someone you love loses their life or gets badly hurt. I've been there, I know. Looking for the silver lining in trauma, abuse, death and horrifying events is incredibly difficult – and often you can't see any positive at all.

Take being shot in the head as an example. What possible good could come from that? Look at Malala Yousafzai. She was a 15-year old schoolgirl who was shot in the head by the Taliban for daring to go to school. Now, Malala is a Nobel peace prize winning activist for education. Being shot in the head has led to incredible, world-shaking things. Certainly not what the Taliban intended when they shot her.

For many of us, adversity will not bring such remarkable changes, but maybe it will bring some benefit – if only the strength, the courage, the resilience to bounce back. Life isn't made up of just terrible, scarring experiences for most of us – there are other negative experiences – job losses, relationship problems, health issues and so on.

I worked at a company in the '90s where many of us talked about leaving on a regular basis. I did leave, but the majority of the others stayed on until the company made redundancies. Then many of the people who had wanted to leave for 5+ years were made redundant. Most of them went on to happier situations, better jobs, more fulfilling roles.

It is scary when something ends. But what if it was all happening *for* you? What if you could trust that life has your back? What if the change in circumstance could be the answer to your prayers? There's no difference in what happens to you, there's just a difference in how it feels – one path leads to worry, ulcers and fear. The other path leads to peace, trust and love.

We don't always know why something is for us when it happens – especially when it seems bad, but maybe you don't need to know? Maybe you just need to trust that life is happening for you, not to you; and in a few years' time, you'll see clearly that the devastating relationship break-up set you free to meet your soulmate.

Tap into the infinite creative well

As recently as 3 years ago, I thought I wasn't that creative. I'd been blogging for years, I'd written 2 ebooks and enough articles to fill 6 books, I'd had all sorts of creative ideas, but I wasn't *creative*. Ok, I could write a bit, but other creative pursuits were off limits as "I'm no good at" them. Then I learnt (thanks to the fabulous Jamie Ridler) it's not about getting it right, it's about expressing your creativity and having fun with it.

Many of us were shut down as kids when we tried something and someone else said it was rubbish. So we stopped doing it, even though we had fun. What a shame. Not only that we stopped having fun, but that we bottled up our creativity just because some pinch-faced fool didn't appreciate our genius. What a shame that we believed that it had to be *good*, that it couldn't just be a first draft or even just a creative outlet.

So we stop creating out of a belief that we're not creative and a fear that we're not good enough to create. Hogwash. Creativity isn't something you are or are not, it's something you tap into - we all have the capacity to create - all we need to do is tap into the infinite creative well.

The Infinite Creative Well

Yes, some people are naturally good painters or writers or sculptors, but you don't have to be naturally good at any creative endeavour to have fun with it. Maybe you can't paint like Picasso, or make music like Mozart, or write like William Shakespeare - but you can be creative in your own way. I bet that there is some creativity in you that is crying out to be expressed. Expressing creativity is not about creating a masterpiece, it's just about allowing your creative energy a chance to come out, to dance, to be joyously allowed.

Let me point something out here - it is an INFINITE creative well. There is no end to it. The more I've created, the more I've allowed myself to tap into the creative well, the more creative fun I've had, the more creative ideas I've had. Allowing yourself to tap into the creative well and have it pour through you is fun, plus the more you practice creativity, the stronger your connection to it gets and the more you can and will do. Many of us have a deep need to create, to express, even if we're not creative or arty. Don't stopper yourself up anymore - let yourself have fun and create.

What creative outlet will you choose next? Painting, drawing, knitting, sewing, crocheting, writing, sculpture, collage, colouring, photography, graphic design, gardening, pottery, jewellery making, singing, dancing, playing an instrument, writing a song, acting. The list of creative activities could go on for hours.

Do it just because it appeals to you. Because it's fun. The more you practice, the more you'll find your creative muscles strengthening. It's so freeing to do something creative - even something you suck at. I started (after having been writing for 7 years) by writing the Morning Pages; then I took a jewellery making class, then I started drawing stick people and learned to use paint.net to make them vibrant and gorgeous.

You've seen some of them in this book. I'm no Serious Artist, let's be honest - who cares? I've had fun, I've made a point, and I may have raised a smile or two. What's next on my creative adventure? I don't know yet, but I do know this fun creative journey will never end. If you haven't already, start yours today - I promise you won't regret it.

Part 3:

Take Charge of

Your Life

Take responsibility for your life (not blame)

One of the things that gets people down the most is feeling powerless. I get it, it was what used to get me down the most. In my mid-twenties I was constantly exhausted, I HATED my job and had done for years, I never had any money; and other than shopping, friends and clubbing, I felt I didn't have anything going for me.

You may spot in that sentence the reasons I never had any money. Ahem. Anyway. The worst thing about it was that I felt completely powerless – it was all happening TO me. Life sucked and *there was nothing I could do*. Right? Er, of course, that's wrong.

It was my life. My job. My energy levels. My debt and spending patterns. I left the job and ran away to the other side of the world. To do so, I had to stop spending every penny, clear my debts and save up. When I did so, I discovered my energy levels improved (it was never sorted fully though, when I came back I was diagnosed with Chronic Fatigue, which a decade later turned out to be MS).

Anyhoo, my point is that when I decided to take responsibility and make some changes, my life changed. While I stayed put, spending money I didn't have on rubbish I didn't need and ignoring my body's cries for help, nothing changed. When I just whined about how much I hated my life, nothing changed.

Funny that. It's YOUR life. Ain't no Knight in Shining Armour going to come clattering into your life on a white steed, Princess. You have to take responsibility for your own life. Make sure you don't take the blame for what you don't like though – it doesn't help you make changes and it feels bad, so it's totally not what this book is about.

I know sometimes it feels like there is nothing you can do. But there are always choices.

1. You can stay where you are and moan (I did this, it's not that effective).

2. Change the situation – talk to your boss about the issues you have; start listening to your body; pay off your debts; sort out the problems that are getting you down.

3. Change yourself. You know when you're in a situation that's driving you INSANE, but someone else in the same situation is breezily sanguine and cheerful? You can do that, it's a learnable skill. Or you can become more assertive, calmer, more accepting. Think

not? Victor Frankl did it, and his situation was way worse; so why not you?

4. Run away to the other side of the world. Or, the slightly less drastic version: leave the situation. If you truly hate your job, and an attitude shift doesn't help, leave it.

Ok, I know it's easy for me to say. I've done all of the above and trust me, it's a lot easier to make changes than to stay miserable, and I know you CAN do it. I have every faith in you. Once you take responsibility for what's going on in your life, you take back your power to DO something about it. It almost doesn't matter what you do, because the very act of taking back your power feels good all by itself.

By the way, unless you are in danger, desperately miserable, or you know that you have to leave in your heart, leaving the situation is the last resort. Even if you plan to leave it *soon*, make changes to make it better anyway. Even if that change is just to lighten up, accept those things you cannot change and be gracious in the situation (it's amazing how often things change by themselves when you do that).

Ultimately, it's your life. You get to decide how to live it. You get to decide to make changes to it if it's not great. As long as you take responsibility. Otherwise, you're at the mercy of a capricious fate/God/whatever you believe in. You may have heard the saying "Life's a bitch and then you die"? Don't live by that – take it in your own hands and do what you need to do to make life a beach instead.

If something bugs you, sort it out

Have you got a wobbly front step? Or squeaky windscreen wipers? Or a niggling debt? Or overflowing cupboards? Or a desk that looks like the paper monster threw up? Or any other irritating thing that bugs you every time you see it?

Sort it out. We all put up with a lot of little things in life that seem to be unimportant – *tomorrow jobs*. Those little things add up to drive you entirely crazy. They tend to be the things that send you over the edge too. On one particularly memorable occasion, I lost my temper over paperclips.

It may not seem that important to fix the dripping tap, or tidy the messy desk, or deal with the gale-force draught blowing through your windows, but those little things have a cumulative effect which drains your energy, drains your joy and eventually drives you barmy. *Little things* stack up to form a tower of stressful stuff.

I used to teach a workshop on stress management, and this exercise was part of the homework: to list all the things you are tolerating and start sorting them out (easiest first). Most people thought this wouldn't make that much difference to their stress levels, but it had a huge impact.

One participant e-mailed me to say how astonished she was at how much difference it made to her energy when she sorted just 3 things that had been irritating her. Once she'd done 20, she reported that she was no longer snapping daily at her colleagues and her husband, and she felt less stressed out than she'd been in months.

Not only was the stress noticeably reduced, but people also reported a rise in energy and in the enjoyment of life. It takes a lot of effort to ignore 100 things that are bugging you. If each one of those 100 things bugs you 6 times a day, eventually you find you are going around with your head perpetually done in.

So, if it's bugging you, fix it. Make a list of things that are irritating you – all those nagging tasks - the car that needs cleaning, calls that need to be returned, you need new knickers, your desk is overflowing with piles of stuff, all those little things that you're planning to sort later; and sort out the easiest one. Then move to the next easiest and so on, until your tower of stress is gone.

Fall down 100 times, get up 101

In Australia in 2001, I did a mountain bike ride down a mountain. They told me it would be easy. They lied. It was hell. The track had been rained on then sun-baked into a teeth-jarring mess, I had to *carry* the bike up a steep incline at one point, and ride down a near vertical narrow pass.

Anyway, when we reached the road, I nearly wept with relief. It was so much easier. Unfortunately, it was also a gravel road and although I saw the pothole in the road ahead, I somehow managed to steer my bike straight into it and fly over the handlebars straight onto my knees. On the gravel.

I'll be honest here, I cried. I howled. I kicked the bike in anger and frustration. Unfortunately, everyone else was about 4 miles ahead and was not there to pick me up and tell me I was being an eejit. So, I picked myself up, picked the gravel out of my knees (ouch), gave myself a hug, and with wobbly legs, got back on the bike and kept going (and, I confess, snivelling).

I learnt three things that day: don't trust the bike shop people (they said it'd be easy); don't go mountain biking on a mountain; and when you fall down, get up, pick the gravel out of your knees, give yourself a hug and keep going.

Life ain't always easy. When you fall down, cry a bit, pick the gravel out of your knees, get a hug and GET BACK UP. So your first ebook bombed? Get up, pick the gravel out of your knees, get a hug and keep writing. So your first business attempt ended in getting a job? Get up, pick the gravel out of your knees and keep entrepreneuring.

If you read autobiographies of successful business bods, you will see in their past: failures, cock-ups and often (surprisingly often) bankruptcy. If you read autobiographies of successful musicians, you will see that often they got rejected and put down and told 'no'. If you read autobiographies of authors, you will see that they often got buried in rejection letters.

You don't have to get rejected or fail - some people succeed first try. I can't think of any right now, but I'm sure they exist. The more likely scenario though is that the path will not be smooth. You will fall down. It's tempting to stay down, crying and showing off the gravel in your knees, but that won't take you forward.

Life doesn't always go the way you hope it will – but rather than falling down and staying down, get back up. You may have to do it a lot. One of my favourite sayings is

"Fall down 100 times, get up 101".

Don't lie in the gravel crying forever. Get up, pick the gravel out of your knees, get a hug (from yourself if there's no one else around) and get back on your bike.

If your bladder's full, go to the toilet

There's a conversation I have with clients fairly often about seeing the signs and using them as a reminder. Like when your bladder is full, you go to the toilet. When your fuel gauge is low, you go to the garage to get fuel. There is no bargaining with the bladder and the fuel tank. You might keep them waiting a little while, but at some point, you are going to have to heed the message and just go to the loo.

Stress, frustration, impatience, tiredness, lack of energy, irritation, lethargy and even procrastination are all the same. They are a message to tell us to do something. Only we put a different meaning on them, or we ignore them altogether. The alternate meaning we usually assign is along the lines of 'I suck'.

"I'm procrastinating, therefore I'm a lazy, good for nothing, idle, useless git."

"Oh my god I'm stressed, I have so much to do, I just need to do 82 things at once. I clearly need to give myself a kick up the ass."

"I've not done x, y, z, what is wrong with me? I must be a terrible person."

"I'm not getting there fast enough, that means I am worthless and I can't do it at all."

"I'm tired. Never mind, more coffee. I don't have time to be tired, I'm far too busy and important (and by extension, I am not worthy of the attention and TLC I clearly need). I slept for at least 3 hours last night, I am just being self-indulgent (which is a bad thing)."

"Oh my god what's wrong with me? I can't get motivated today, I just want to go back to bed and throw the duvet over my head. I am such a waste of space."

Recognise any of those scripts? You may have your own version of them – I encourage you to notice over the next week or two what your habitual response is to tiredness, procrastination, stress, low energy, frustration etc. I'm going to take a wild stab in the dark and suggest it's not a positive, helpful response. It's probably going to be some form of self-deprecation or self-criticism. If it's not, I congratulate you, you're a rare bird.

For most of us, our habitual responses aren't about reading the signs and acting upon them (bladder full = toilet; empty fuel gauge = go fill up with fuel). Instead, we ignore them, try to push through them, get irritated with the sign itself, or make it about the sign "I'm such a grouch"; "I always procrastinate"; "I am so frustrated with life", instead of looking deeper and asking what that sign is showing you.

The full bladder shows you that you need to go to the bathroom. The parched mouth shows you that you need water. The empty fuel tank says you need fuel. You don't go around saying "I have such a full bladder, I have a terribly low capacity for fluid" (unless you have a very small bladder). You don't say "I have such a dry mouth, I only drank last Thursday, I don't understand why I'm thirsty AGAIN". You don't consider your car lazy or self-indulgent for needing fuel once in a while.

They're just signs that point you to very clear solutions. As will your stress, impatience, procrastination, tiredness, low energy, irritation, lethargy and all the other signs you're currently ignoring or not investigating. The solutions may not be as simple as 'drink water', 'go to the toilet' or 'fill with fuel'; but they also may well be that simple *once you understand them*.

For me, if I'm procrastinating it's usually either because I don't want to do whatever it is OR I haven't decided what I'm going to do (so I just fart about on Facebook for a few hours). If I'm frustrated and impatient, I usually need to take some action (instead of whinging about nothing happening). If I'm stressed, I need to take a breath and step away from the desk for a dance break or a walk.

If I'm tired, lethargic, or have low energy, these could mean one of a few things: I need a snooze because I need sleep, I need a dance break because I need energy, I need an afternoon off because I'm feeling burned out, I need time out to refuel, or I need some TLC because I've not been taking great care of myself.

If I'm irritated, it's a sign that either I need some self-care OR I have forgotten to take my Vitamin B6 and Evening Primrose. I get really bad PMT and if I don't take my supplements, I'm exceedingly irritable and short-tempered. My friends and family are so very glad that I've got better at reading this particular sign.

What about you? What signs are you not seeing? Where are you criticising yourself unfairly for something that is a symptom, not a cause? Where are you pushing on regardless of your empty fuel tank and full bladder? What are these things trying to tell you and show you?

Trust me, these are questions worth answering, because not only do you stop bitching at yourself, you also experience less frustration, stress, irritation and lethargy. Maybe because you remember to take your pills, or maybe because you are doing what works. If your bladder is full, go to the toilet.

Throw out the shoulds

Indulge me for a moment here. I want you to do a little exercise – list 20 'should's – 20 things you think you should do. Now, how do you feel? Inspired? Good about yourself? Joyous? Ready to run right now and tackle the should-do list? Or flat, fed up, down on yourself, uninspired, and feeling like you'd rather poke your eyes out with a stick than do any of those things?

Here's the thing about 'should' – it's demotivating, and it doesn't work. You can tell yourself all year long that you *should* go to the gym, but if you don't want to, you won't. Now take a look at your list and change the 'I should' to 'I want to'. If any of them don't ring true – i.e.

you don't want to at all, cross them off the list. If you *have to* do them, change it from 'I should' to 'I have to' and go do it.

Watch out for the sneaky shoulds – the ones that put jackboots on and pretend to be 'have to's: Feed the baby? Yes, that's a 'have to'. Go to the gym? No, this is not a 'have to' – that one is a should with jackboots on. Do you want to go to the gym? No? Then get it off the list.

Stop wasting your time and energy and precious self-confidence on things you don't have to do and don't want to do. You may genuinely feel you should go to the gym because you want to get fit. However, if you don't really want to go to the gym, you'll resist and you won't go.

This is a total waste of time and is not getting you what you want. What you really want is to get fit. You can do that by walking in the park, by dancing, by playing tennis with a friend, by setting up obstacle courses in the garden with the kids.

The shoulds distract you from the action you *could* be taking to get what you really want. Get rid of them. This is your life. If you have to beat yourself with the birch twig of 'should', you're missing a better way to do it. Find the 'want to' and do that. Tap into your desire instead.

Many of us treat ourselves as if we were naughty schoolchildren who need to be nagged and pushed and hounded into doing what is good for us. Actually, we don't. Most of us want what is good for us, but we resist the things we think we should do. Rightly so. Because if it's a should, it's not a want.

Or maybe it is a want that's been buried under layers of bullshit and shame for not doing it because we've been badgering ourselves about it for so long. It's time to stop shoulding all over yourself. If for no other reason, because it doesn't work. If you're anything like me, you'll have an inner rebellious teenager who will resist like a herd of mules any pushing to do something you don't want to.

That inner rebellious teenager is a gift – she's telling you there's a better way to get the best from yourself. It's not guilt, obligation, and shame (funnily enough). It's desire, want, freedom to choose your path. Try it – find what the want is behind the should, and see how much better that works for you.

Get clear what you want in life

If you're anything like me, you grew up understanding that you got a good education, then a good job, a good house, spouse and car, an effing big television, and all the other trappings of the suburban life. If this vision makes your heart sing, good for you, keep going down that road.

However, if like me, you want something different, (or if you've got all that, and you still feel like there must be more to life), you need to start getting clear about exactly what you do want from your life. Don't get too neurotic and stressed about it. It's easy to start going into some kind of angsty headless chicken search of tragic proportions (I did. That's why I'm advising you not to bother, it doesn't help you find what you want, and it's ridiculous).

The quest for a life you love is a very personal and wonderful journey. Yes, we all want to know NOW what we want, but that attitude will just get in your way (trust me, I know). Approach it with an attitude of joyous curiosity, treat it as a beautiful journey of discovery – a treasure hunt.

Along the way, you will turn down roads you realise are not for you, and that's ok. You will turn down cul-de-sacs, and that's ok too. Every dead-end, every realisation about what is not for you helps you learn what is for you, and what you really want. The search for the life you want is actually an inside job, not a search for something outside.

Sometimes we're just not ready to see what's inside – it's buried so deeply that we need to follow the clues, like a trail of breadcrumbs, until one day we realise we knew what we were looking for all along. Everything that brings you to that point is valuable and interesting and worth experiencing.

Like the years I spent bouncing around the various departments in my corporate life. I tried over a dozen jobs on for size and couldn't settle to any one of them. As it turned out when I started running my own business, it was useful to have a really good understanding of how the back office of a company works and thorough training in accounts and IT. I didn't know it at the time, but it was all invaluable experience that many business owners struggle without.

This phase of searching and figuring out what you want is such a wonderful phase. I missed all the wonder and joy in it because I was just desperate to know what I should do with *the rest of my life* (at 25 years old - talk about taking myself too seriously). Looking back, I can see what a marvellous phase it was – to seek and discover and explore and inquire and quest.

And I cannot recommend highly enough getting a coach to help you with this one. It's our job to help you get what your true heart's desire is and remove all your objections to having it (the 'oh I couldn't possibly's and 'I am not worthy's and 'I can't do that's). Yes, you can figure this all out alone, but why not entertain the idea of getting some help and support?

My first coach got me started on this path of coach, business-woman and writer. When I think back, I can't believe where the path has led me; and I wouldn't have believed it back then either. So, if you haven't already, start figuring out what you really want from your life.

This is not what you thought you wanted, or what you wanted when you were 12 or 20, or what you think you *should* want, or what someone else wants for you, but what YOU really want. Because loving your life is going to involve living the life you truly want with all your heart.

Go after what you want

Once you know what you want, go after it. Take baby steps in the direction of the life you truly want. This is how people who have amazing lives got them. They went after them. I know that sounds like I'm pointing out the bleeding obvious, but sometimes we think people are just lucky, or their lives randomly turned out wonderful while ours went randomly tits up.

It's not really so. Some people do fall into an amazing life that they love, but they will have made some choices, tried some things, put themselves in the road to be run over by opportunity (metaphorically) and taken some action to get to that amazing life. They also might just have a great attitude that helped them to turn crap into diamonds. So try. Risk failure. Reach for the life you want.

I know that can be a super scary idea. Change is scary, and you may have had the belief that things would just happen for you. So if they didn't, the idea of going out and making things happen can be terrifying. What if you fail? But dying inside is way worse than failing, trust me.

It's true, you might fail, you might not get what you're going after. So what? That's not as big a deal as you think. Trying will bring you more gifts than I can tell you about – confidence, experience, joy, exhilaration, energy, aliveness, the knowledge that at least you tried and had the courage to have a go. Yes, the downsides exist too – the fear, the lack of self-belief, the obstacles and roadblocks.

Even those *bad* things turn out to be good – because you come across those problems so you can solve them. This makes you stronger and more confident and gives you even more skills to take through life with you. Yeah, I admit, sometimes it sucks and it hurts and you get nostalgic for a safe, boring, caged life.

But it never hurts as badly as living in that cage (of your own making). Nothing hurts more than living a life you don't enjoy, wishing it could be different and feeling trapped in it. So once you know what you want, go for it. The big stuff, the little stuff, the everyday stuff, the once-in-a-lifetime stuff. It's all waiting to be experienced.

Going after what you want in life is exhilarating, fun, stretches you (in a good way), and makes you feel ALIVE. There's the added bonus that if you try, you might just get what you want. (If you don't go after what you want, you definitely won't get it, right?)

One word of warning here: this book is about loving your life, right? So there's no need to do this from a place of stress and need and drive and 'if I don't get this my life is ovvvveeeerrrr'. Come from a place of curiosity and joyful desire. Dance towards what you want with a light heart and bright hope, don't trudge grimly through life desperately seeking something better.

You don't have to be stupid about it, like I was, and make a wild leap into the unknown with no parachute. You can just baby step your way into a life you love, tiptoeing past your fears into the life you've dreamed off.

"A journey of a thousand miles begins with a single step" – Lao Tzu

Take that single step. Then take the next one. And keep doing that. It's that simple. Not always easy, but that simple. Of course, if you need help, I recommend you get a coach for this – that's what gave me the support and inspiration I needed to move into a life I love.

Be prepared to fall on your arse

"Life is one continuous mistake" – Dogen Zenji (Japanese Zen Buddhist teacher)

How prepared to mess up are you? Are you terrified of failure? Are you afraid to try in case you mess up? Are you playing it so safe that you never try anything new? Are you happy to be wrong? Our fear of failure is strong, but only while we hold ourselves in stasis, not daring to risk failure.

Once we've failed a few times, it's no longer such a big deal. It doesn't kill you. It actually helps you succeed. As Peter Jones of Dragon's Den says "Failure's just feedback". Mastery of any task is not achieved in one try. It is done by trying over and over and over and getting it wrong until you get it right. Athletes don't become gold-medallists the first time they try their event. They practice, they improve, and then they win.

Businesswomen don't spring from the womb with an entrepreneurial manual for how to do business right. They learn through trial and error. Mostly error. Scratch the surface of any successful business bod and you will find a business mess up in their past. Often more than one.

When you learned to walk, you fell on your bottom often in the beginning. It's part of learning something new that you will fall on your bum. If you're not prepared to do that, you'll never learn to walk. Failure isn't as horrifying as we fear. Many of us are utterly terrified of it; then it happens and the world doesn't end. It sucks, sure, but it's just failure.

Failure is not who you are, it doesn't make you a bad person, it doesn't mean you're a loser. It just means you fell on your backside. Frankly, I'd rather have the guts to have a go, than to sit on the sidelines mocking others for trying something I wouldn't dare try. (Theodore Roosevelt said it better in his "The Man in the Arena" speech – google it if you've never heard it.)

What happened the last time you failed? Were you inspired to keep going? Or did you stop because you'd failed? Stopping is what most people do – think of New Year's Resolutions that get dumped by the 9th of January. Because we've fallen off the wagon a couple of times by then, most of us will at that point give up.

But you can just treat whatever you're trying to do as an experiment. Evaluate your experiment. What worked, what totally didn't work, what could you improve on to make it easier for yourself to succeed? This is not what most of us do. We try something. We perceive that we fail. We stop trying.

We try again (often doing exactly the same thing as last time). We perceive that we fail again. We stop trying, now beating ourselves up for being 50 shades of useless. So the pattern continues. Maybe we start to notice (after the 8th failed experiment) that there is something we could tweak that would work a lot better and help us to succeed.

If we treat each attempt with curiosity instead of a critical eye, we can pick up these small tweaks and potential improvements more quickly. We would also miss out the self-flagellation that adds to our sense of failure and disappointment in ourselves for trying and missing the mark.

Nothing you try is ever wasted because you learn from it - if you allow yourself to. If you just aim for perfection and fall short of your own unrealistic expectations, you undermine yourself some more. That just doesn't help.

So don't do it.

Fall on your arse, get back up and stick up two fingers at the idea that failure is the worst thing that can happen. It's not. Never failing is, because it means you're not trying. Staying safe is tempting, it seems easy (although your soul will be screaming), and you won't fail.

Only you will. You'll fail to live fully, completely, the way you truly can live. You'll fail to discover the depth of your brilliance.

"Success is stumbling from failure to failure with no loss of enthusiasm" – Winston Churchill

If you're not prepared to make mistakes, you are not prepared to grow and create and have fun and do new things; and you can't fall in love with a life that is that constrained.

"If you stumble, make it part of the dance" - Unknown

It's part of the dance of life to stumble, to mess up, to fail, to fall on your arse. Keep on dancing through life like that's exactly what you meant to do. Be prepared to fall on your arse again and again. That way you'll learn, you'll become brave and you'll be able to take higher and higher leaps. And one day you won't fall, you'll fly.

You don't need to wake the sleeping lion

You may have heard some version of this idea:

"Move out of your comfort zone. You can only grow if you are willing to feel awkward and uncomfortable when you try something new." Brian Tracy

"Life begins at the end of your comfort zone." Neale Donald Walsch

While to an extent I agree with this sentiment, I like to put it a slightly different way: Just *lean against the edge of your comfort zone.* Whistling. (The whistling is optional.)

The point is, sometimes leaping out of our comfort zone is, well, uncomfortable. Or terrifying and it freaks us out. So we don't leap. Or we try and it's too scary so we scuttle back into the centre of the comfort zone and vow never to leave again.

I call it 'waking the sleeping lion'. Your fears are a sleeping lion. If you go too far out of your comfort zone, the lion wakes up, roars, and bites your head off. If you just lean against the edge of your comfort zone, whistling softly, the lion has no reason to wake up and roar. This way, you expand your comfort zone gently, easily and without so much stress.

If you're happy leaping out of your comfort zone, go for it. But if you're afraid of the sleeping lion, try this – just lean against the edge of your comfort zone. Think of something you'd love to do that is outside your comfort zone. Now take a teeny, tiny baby step towards it. Make a call, look it up on Auntie Google, make a plan, buy something you'll need, just do something small.

Then take another baby step, and keep baby stepping. Soon (sooner than you think) you'll find that you've expanded your comfort zone to include whatever it was you wanted to do, or that thing now lies just outside your comfort zone, and only needs another little lean to the edge to get there.

The life you really really love probably does lie outside your comfort zone, because one of the things we need to love life is to be challenged in some way, and that can be uncomfortable. You don't have to make it painful and difficult, you can just lean, gently against your edge. Whistling.

There are no problems, only solutions

This is one of my dad's favourite sayings. Although I find it a bit irritating when I'm busy having a problem, I agree with the sentiment wholeheartedly. Very few problems have no solution (unfortunately they're usually the biggies), most problems have many possible solutions. If only we'd stop focusing on the problem long enough to look for a solution.

I have noticed a disorder among my clients that I've dubbed Problem Powerlessness Paralysis. Here are the symptoms:
- complain about the problem
- blame everyone else
- feel utterly powerless
- become adamant that there is no solution to be found
- get stuck entirely in the problem and how awful it is

Do you recognise any of those symptoms? I do the same thing when in the grip of PPP. Luckily we have a fix for the syndrome – Creative Solutions Brainstorm. It is amazing what a change comes over clients when they move from PPP to CSB – they feel freer, more in charge of their lives, more optimistic, they stop complaining and blaming and they get unstuck.

Sometimes just knowing there's the possibility of a solution is enough to jolt you out of PPP. The question I always use with anyone stuck in PPP is this: **So, what can you do?**

There's always something that can be done. Even in the most impossible "it's not me it's them" situations, there's always something YOU can do. (Just for the record, it's very rarely just them.) It may be an attitude adjustment, it may be an action you can take, and it may be that you need to take yourself out of the situation.

Even global problems have solutions. They may not be easy, they may need the co-operation of millions of people, but the solutions are there. Most of us aren't trying to bring about world peace or end poverty though, so our problems are infinitely more fixable. Still, the more thorny issues might take time and effort over years to solve. Does that mean you don't bother trying?

Not if you really want a solution. If you want to solve the problem, you'll do what you need to do to solve it. Even if it's not an instantaneous fix, even if you have to try different ideas, even if you have to bring all your creative skills to the table. A problem is just a puzzle to be solved, and the more you can see it in that curious, interested way, the easier you will find it to solve your problems.

Sometimes the problem on the surface isn't the real problem. Like when you get headaches because you need glasses. Or you have insomnia because you're worried about your loved ones. The real problem isn't always the one you see. Sometimes what you see is just the symptom, not the real cause. So drill down, find the real problem and solve that.

My friend had all manner of symptoms, including weight gain, depression, skin problems, and digestive issues. She was offered a variety of solutions to those problems, which *couldn't* work because the underlying problem that was causing all those other problems wasn't fixed. Once she went on an elimination diet, ALL of the problems cleared up. So make sure you're finding the solution to the real problem, not just the symptoms.

There's a saying in one of Raymond E Feist's books "Life is problems. Living is solving problems." You may have noticed that already – life is problems. Shit happens. Cars break down, jobs change, bosses turn into boss-zilla, relationships end, and so on. So the more comfortable you can get with finding solutions, the easier your life will be.

It's hard to love life when you are weighed down by endless problems you don't know how to solve, so get your jazzy creative pants on and have some fun with finding the answers to the puzzles.

If you don't know how to solve a problem, you'll figure it out. You don't have to do it alone, you can ask other people for help too – two heads are better than one, right?

Make your dreams come true every day

What have you always wanted to do or have or be? Make a list. Now go do the easiest thing. There's probably something super easy you can do within the next month. Go do it, get it, be it. Put it in your diary, drag someone else along with you for accountability, make a plan to make sure you do it, save for it, order it. Make one of those dreams come true.

Don't wait for when you're retired. Do the stuff you want to do now. Make your life about making dreams come true, not about working for 40+ years so that you can maybe make a dream come true later, in some imaginary future. By then, you may have forgotten your dreams, or you may (and probably will) have changed and no longer want the same things.

Ok, a lot of our dreams are BIG, so it's the work of more than a day to make them come true, but you CAN work on them every day. Want to write a book? Write every day. Want to travel the world? Start a savings account and add to it every day with your spare change. Want to start your own business? Work on it every day.

See, **your dreams are yours to heed or ignore**. You may have a partner who makes your 'go to Paris in spring' dream come true, but they can't write your book or paint your masterpieces. You have to do it. Too many of us wait until we have more money; the kids are older; we have kids and will have more time (collective pause for the Moms reading to have hysterics); we have a less stressful job; we are older; less tired; more confident; have a personality transplant.

The truth is that these excuses are all bull. Not just the 'more time when you have kids' one. How long have you been putting your dreams on hold for? Not just BIG dreams either, small dreams that you never seem to get around to. There's a painting by Ira Mitchell-Kirk called "Jump for Joy" that I adore – the first time I saw it in a Facebook post I fell in love with it.

My friend sent me a card with it on that I promptly framed and put on the wall. I kept telling myself that *one day*, I'd get a print of it. Today I was having a dance break before writing (my top writing tip for you there) and I suddenly decided that now was a really good time to go get the print. So today, I made that dream come true.

That mini dream is a year old, and it took less than 10 minutes to fulfil. You're the dreamweaver in your life. You're the fairy godmother you've been waiting for. You're the ones with the reins of the Wild Horse of Dreams. Ride that horse. Make your dreams come true – big ones, little ones, in between ones. Fun ones, serious ones, 25-year-old ones, born yesterday ones. Make your dreams come true. Every day of your magical life.

Follow your big dreams

While we're on the subject of making dreams come true, let's just dip into the sub-section of BIG dreams. You know, those dreams that leave your heart beating a little fast, and your brain going 'how the heck are you going to do *that*?' The ones that are so big you're not even sure where to start or whether they're even possible.

The ones that frighten you a bit (or a lot). The ones that bring up all the 'I couldn't possibly's and 'who? Me?'s. The dreams that seem impossible at first glance, but just won't let you go. The ones that even after you've dismissed them as fantasy, just keep coming back and whispering to you. The dreams that even if you can't hear them anymore, you know they're still there, hiding in your heart.

Here's the thing about Big Dreams: there are no certainties. There's no guarantee they'll come true. They bring with them the potential to hurt you and the potential to fail. They also bring the potential for magic and miracles and wonder and for becoming the very best you that you can be. Because Big Dreams stretch you, they make you go places you wouldn't if you didn't follow them.

You'll have heard the phrase "it's the journey that matters, not the destination" – and that's why you must follow your Big Dreams, even with the spectre of failure hanging over your head. Because the journey alone makes it worth taking the trip. The end result is an added bonus that you'll thoroughly enjoy - for just a short time before a new Big Dream comes bubbling up.

This may make it sound a bit pointless and meaningless, but truly the joy, the fun, the growth, the adventure, the stretching, the learning, the curiosity, the fascination come from the journey. Sometimes we get so focused on the Big Dream, we miss the magnificence of the journey.

When I was seeking my dream, seeking my future, seeking the thing that would make my life pop, I missed that those years were a joyful adventure of discovery. I completely missed it because I was so desperate to find my purpose. Now, as I look back, I can see what fun it was, what joy it held, what wonderment I was completely oblivious to.

Still, I learned the lesson, and now, even when my current Big Dream seems a million miles away, I remember that the reason to follow the Big Dream is for the journey it will take me on. That Big Dream, whatever it is, has come to you for a reason. It's in your heart for a reason. If you follow it, you'll have an adventure, you'll learn, you'll grow, you'll become more confident, you'll have more fun than if you didn't follow it.

When you follow your Big Dreams, you are following the true North of your soul. The compass is pointing you towards where you truly need to go. When you go that way, it feels so right. Even when it looks wrong, and other people are busy questioning your choices, and it's not working out as you expected, it still feels like the right path.

You don't have to know exactly how you'll get there, you just need to set foot on the path and start the journey. It'll take you on the ride of your life. I could go on about this subject for hours, and indeed I have, in my podcast "Dreams to Reality" – so if you are ready to start a Big Dream journey and you want some help and inspiration, you can find the podcast on donnaonthebeach.com.

Get rid of whatever's holding you back

When I talk to clients about their vision for their life, their heart's desires, their dreams, we always find things that are getting in their way. Obstacles. Blockages. Fears and beliefs that stop them from moving forward. "It's not possible for someone like me to do x" for example.

Let me repeat that. We ALWAYS find things that are getting in their way. Not sometimes, not occasionally, not once in a while. Always. These blockages can be ridiculous, they can be minor, and they can be a huge Sherman tank the other side of a barbed wired fence, around a castle manned by knights shooting arrows. They can be understandable, they can be clear, they can be sneaky – disguised as something else.

They're very likely to exist. Am I telling you this to discourage you and make you give up on your best life? Of course not, I am telling you so that you know it's not just you. Everyone who ever achieved anything had obstacles and blockages in their way. There is no difference between them and you – they just got past their obstacles and blockages.

There are always obstacles and blockages, and that is a good thing. Because *obstacles are not there to stop us*. They are there to show us something. To show us where we need to develop and grow and gain confidence. To show us how we can become bigger, better, faster, stronger. To show us where there is something we need to learn.

The better we get at interpreting those signs, the easier the path becomes. The more obstacles we get over, under, around and through, the less they slow us down because we gain the muscles to just punch on through. Obstacles, blockages, fears, beliefs that don't help you, and doubts exist. Getting past them makes you stronger, more resilient, and more confident.

It builds your muscles for the next big adventure in your life. Obstacles and blockages help you to move forward because when you get past them, you're better able to get past the next ones. Sometimes the same things come up again and again. Every time I work on a creative project, I wonder if it's any good. The first few times, I would chew on the fear it wasn't any good for months.

I would allow that fear to stop me for months. I would lose confidence in myself and my work. Eventually, my natural tenacity (stubbornness) would re-assert itself and I would pick myself up, dust myself off, re-read what I'd done, realise I'm a genius and keep going. Now, when that fear comes up that it's no good, I recognise it.

I'm almost at the point of saying 'oh hi, it's you. Welcome. Your arrival means I'm hitting the outer edge of my comfort zone, and that's exciting.' I say almost. It happened with this project and I ran into my metaphorical cave and didn't work on this for a couple of weeks.

I had made progress though because I didn't chew on the fear for months, I just wandered away to have some time off. After the fear had receded, I realised I had hit a growth edge and it was a) exciting and b) part of the process I've been through 15 times and therefore No Big Deal.

The first few times you hit snags, you struggle. Then you get a bit blasé because you've seen it before. You've got through a crisis of confidence. You've climbed over a wall of despair. You've knocked down a fear of failure. I tell clients there is a treasure map with X marking the spot of their desires. To get there they have to go through the mountains of worry, the forest of doubt, the castle of uncertainty, the swamp of fear, the river of under-confidence, and the desert of failure. Maybe you have some more terrors of your own making too.

The first time you go through them, it's scary. But you get there. The next time it's not scary, it's just the river of under-confidence. You'll get across it. You might be half a mile downriver, but you'll get across. You know this because you gained confidence by doing it before. Every time you do it, it gets easier, and you do start to enjoy the challenge because you know that challenge means progress.

It doesn't mean "Stop! Go No Further. There Be Dragons in These Mountains." It just means you have some stuff to do, to overcome, to clear out, to build up. It just means you have to find a way over, under, round or through those obstacles. You can do that because you're resourceful and fabulous (I know this, you wouldn't have got this far in this book if you weren't).

So, what's holding you back? Give it a name, describe it. Trust your inner wisdom to know what it is and what it's about. Now get rid of that obstacle. You can get help.[1] You can get support and advice and coaching and cuddles and cheerleading and kicks up the behind.

Now you've found something that's holding you back, find your way under it, over it, round it or just through it. Get rid of it. Moreover, don't worry if it comes back again – you've got past it once, you can and you will again. Eventually, you will say 'oh hi, it's you' and breeze on past like there was nothing in the way of what you want.

The monster under the bed is normally just a sock

Fear can paralyse you, can stop you from doing anything new with your life, can stop you from trying things, and can stop you from enjoying your life, because you're too afraid to change or to try. Don't let this happen to you. Most of what we're afraid of never happens. Those things that do, it turns out, we can deal with.

Sometimes we feel like we're the only forty-something year old that gets scared or insecure. It's not just you. I've been coaching for over a decade now and almost everyone I've worked with has had some fear of something. Especially when it comes to change, to trying new things, to leaning out of their comfort zone. It's normal.

What we tend to do is magnify the fear. Like a little kid who's convinced there is a monster hiding under the bed, we're convinced

---

[1] I have a book on this very subject, called 'Obstacle Busting' – it's available on Amazon.

that whatever we want to do is utterly terrifying and a monster. But it's usually just a sock. If you have a phobia about socks, this is not going to help, but I think that's pretty rare.

For the rest of us, it helps to remember that the monster under the bed is just a sock. It's not terrifying and life-threatening. It's just a sock. It's no big deal. I used to be petrified of public speaking. Then I joined Toastmasters (a wonderful organisation that teaches you to be a better, more confident public speaker) and although the first few times I had to speak, I was shaking; it turned out that it wasn't that scary. It was just a sock.

Now the idea of public speaking makes me a little nervous, certainly, but I'm not reduced to a quivering blushing jelly anymore. Because it isn't that scary. The first time I shared one of my (rubbish) drawings, I was afraid. Now, the first thing I do when I finish one is to share it on Facebook. If you'd told me that a few months ago, I'd have called the men in white coats out to you.

Turned out, the terrifying monster under the bed was just a sock. Again. Almost every scary monster thing I've done – travelling to the other side of the world on my own, starting a business, that first coaching client, my first blog post, my first book, the first video I recorded, the first podcast I recorded et cetera et cetera – they've all turned out to be a sock.

The only thing I can think of that really was a monster was jumping out of a plane. I'm scared of flying. Also heights. And falling from 12000 feet. So that was a fairly stupid thing to do. But I know people (like the mad Aussie I had strapped to my back for the jump) who think jumping out of a plane is not scary at all. It's just a sock.

Don't let fear get in the way of you having an amazing life. You can get scared, and you will. Just don't let it stop you, because one day you'll look back and see that what you were afraid of really wasn't that scary after all. It was just a sock.

Don't try to change your entire life in one go

I know you have a hundred things you want to change or do in your life, so why work on one goal when you can work on 300 simultaneously? Of course, as you know wise reader, when you're working on 300 things at once, your attention is scattered, you're overwhelmed, stressed, tired, there's no time to do anything, and you don't make discernible progress on any of those 300 things, which makes you feel bad, discourages you and makes you wonder what the point of it all is.

How often do you make a decision that you will sort everything in your life out at once, live like a Trappist monk for 3 days and then fall spectacularly off the wagon? I used to do it every January (which I've since realised is the WORST time of year for me to change anything – it's the depths of winter, I'm busy hibernating).

We all do it. We want to sort out an area of life (or our entire life) and we go gung-ho at it like a soldier at the charge of the Light Brigade. Unfortunately, it doesn't often work that well. Changing our lives means changing behaviour, underlying habits, underlying beliefs, clearing any resistance to change, and many more things that we fail to take into account when we decide to repay ALL our debts this week, and start 5 savings accounts, and increase our income 7-fold immediately.

And then we fail. Sadly at that point, most of us give up, at least temporarily. What's the point of trying if we just fail over and over again? That's a real shame because we could succeed if we just changed our focus from changing everything to changing just a few small things.

Last year, I was busy making no progress on about 16 financial goals. Then I realised that trying to make 16 different financial goals happen all at once is stupid, so I decided to change my focus. I picked the top 3 financial goals and decided to focus solely on them for now. Within a week, I'd achieved all 3 of those goals.

To be clear, these were all fairly short-term goals, but I wasn't really sure how I was going to accomplish them in a month, never mind in a week. You see, something magical happens when you focus your attention:

The universe aligns in your favour.

Honestly, it does – I know that sounds like woo-woo clap-trap, but it genuinely does.

"Once you make a decision, the universe conspires to make it happen" - Ralph Waldo Emerson.

In the week after I made the decision to just focus on 3 small goals, several things just fell into place in what appeared to be a miraculous way – money I didn't know I had appeared, refunds I didn't know were coming appeared, things I needed to buy were cheaper than I had expected, expensive events I was due to go to were cancelled. Lots of things conspired to help me hit 3 financial goals in a week.

By stopping myself from trying to do 16 things at once, I gave myself the space and the focus to achieve 3. By the end of the same month, another 3 had been accomplished and I was onto the next 3. Just by taking small steps on a couple of short term goals.

Those small steps DO add up, but if your focus is scattered around 68 different projects, you cannot see any changes happening. When you focus on one goal, one area of life, one small change, it is much easier to see the change.

So what will you focus in on this week? Just choose one thing, maybe two if they're low maintenance, and focus on getting that one thing done, or changing that one behaviour (chocolate biscuits after every meal anyone?), or taking small steps towards that one goal. You will start to see the universe move to meet you, you'll start accomplishing your goals, which will increase your confidence and help you do more. It's a virtuous circle.

You're allowed to change your mind

One of my friends has always had a hard time with me being such a flake – every time we spoke I had a new hare-brained idea, a new passion, a new obsession. I moved from accountancy to IT, I ran off to Australia for a year, I started a journalism course (I sucked), I decided to study massage therapy, I was enthused by coaching. There was always some new thing that caught my butterfly-like attention.

He felt this was a bad thing. That I should pick something and stick to it. Uh-huh. That was never going to happen. So instead we kept having conversations where he would say 'so, how's x going?' and I'd be like 'oh my god, that's so last week dahling'. His eye would start to twitch and I'd get a lecture about sticking to something.

Actually, I wasn't quite that flaky, and I'd only say 'that's so last week' if I was being sarcastic. But it is a fair distillation of 30 conversations over 4 years or so. I wasn't deliberately trying to be flaky though. I was trying to find my place in the world. I made some mistakes. The accountancy course can still render me comatose with boredom just thinking about the "management information module". SNORE.

If I had followed said friend's advice, I would still be stuck on the management information module, trying to think of a better answer to the question 'why do managers need information' than 'because they don't know' (seems blindingly obvious to me, but in that course you needed to write 1000's of words about it).

Here's the truth of the matter: I changed my mind about accountancy. I also changed my mind about journalism, IT and a host of other random ideas I tried. I'm allowed to change my mind. I've changed my mind a million times about a million things. I know I've said it a lot, but this is your life – you're allowed to make decisions about it. Even if that involves changing your mind.

Even if it means dealing with the consequences of dropping out, leaving a relationship or changing careers. This seems like a good point to make a distinction: there's a difference between changing your mind because it's what's right for you and your life, and just changing your mind on a whim. Impulsive and irrational behaviour isn't what I'm talking about here.

This is about the deep knowing in your heart that this is the right thing for you. It might look like impulsive and irrational behaviour to other people, but as long as you have the courage of your convictions their opinions are irrelevant. I do not regret stopping the accountancy course, no matter how good a job it would have led to, no matter how exasperated my colleagues and certain friends were with me because I knew it was right.

You need to be able to change your mind. Without that, you end up in a loveless marriage for 10 years before you can escape, or a job that stifles your soul, or doing a course for 4 years that makes you want to weep in bored frustration. Yes, yes, the ability to follow an idea through to completion is good, and if you are one of those lucky folk who knows from the age of 15 what you wish to do with the next 80 years of your life, good for you. I'm not disputing that keeping your word or following a thing through to completion is good. (I'm finishing this book, am I not?)

It is also a good thing to be flexible, to change your mind when you realise that actually, you don't want that bloke/job/career. It's a good thing to know your own mind – it shows strength and decisiveness and confidence (even if some people mistake it for weakness). You're allowed to change your mind. And you will, many times in your life.

I no longer think that Duran Duran are the best band in the world. I no longer believe that the boy I fancied when I was 13 is the hottest guy alive. I changed my mind. I'm glad I did. Because I want to live my life on what's right for me now, not on decisions I made when I didn't know better. If you think about it, nor do you.

Part 4:

Be The Best Friend

You Ever Had

Be fully, beautifully, unashamedly YOU

You're the only you in all creation. Be that. Fully and completely. Don't try to pretend you're anything you're not. Be YOU. Fully, unashamedly, beautifully YOU. The more you that you can be, the more joy you will find because it's no fun being un-you. It's no fun trying to be a social butterfly if at heart you're a hermit. It's no fun trying to pretend to be smashie nicie if you're sarcastic.

It takes guts to be fully, beautifully, unashamedly YOU. It is a hard thing in a world where conformity is the name of the game to stand up and say "this is me – with all my weirdness and oddities and geekiness hanging out". Most people are not fully, beautifully, unashamedly themselves. Most of us hide parts of who we are out of a fear of being seen as weird or odd or different.

We're all weird and odd and different. We're unique. Each one of us is the only me in all creation. Whenever we hide a piece of that uniqueness, you not only deny yourself, you deny the whole world the pleasure of who you really are.

Have you ever wondered why we're attracted to authenticity? Because when people aren't hiding, they're gorgeous. Yeah, some people won't like your brand of dazzle, but who gives a monkey's? Real, genuine people shine – they're beautiful.

And despite the weird social pressure to conform and fit in, we know that's bull. We don't like fake, we don't like phoney. You don't often hear of someone being praised for being a fake, or being lauded for being a sheep. "Oh, I love that woman, she's so conformist." Nope, never going to happen. Unless you happen to be a dictator who wants everyone to conform to your world view of course.

You are unique. You are your own brand of genius. If you could only see how wonderful you are, how special, how you do not need to hide away. You are enough for the life you want. But you'll need every bit of you for it. You'll need to be fully, beautifully, unashamedly you.

I know that's hard for some of us. Especially if we've got some odd vision of what Perfect Me looks like. She's probably got really shiny hair, doesn't lose her temper or her keys, is elegant, confident, serene, fabulous at everything she turns her hand to, never makes a fashion mistake or goes out with an unsuitable man and always knows what to do.

Am I right? I got news for you babe, that woman doesn't exist. If you keep trying to live up to that impossible ideal, you will miss the fact that you with your messy hair, scatterbrain, old comfy jeans, your blushing cheeks and your mistake making…YOU are 120 times the woman that plastic airhead will ever be.

Clear the dust off the diamond that is you and let yourself shine – be fully, beautifully, unashamedly YOU.

Be who you want to be today

Who do you want to be? Not a specific who, like Beyoncé (I mean, who wouldn't want to be her - girl's got it going on), a type of person who. Do you want to be light, joyful, happy, peaceful, calm, confident, sexy?

Be that then.

Start now, today to be the person you want to be.

We're all fond of saying "when x happens, I shall be happier/sexier/more fun/calmer/etc.", but why wait? If you want to be calmer, be calmer today, not when you're living in a convent. If you want to be happier, get happier today, not when everything in your life is exactly as you want it to be (never gonna happen). If you want to be sexier, be sexier now, not when you've lost x pounds.

It's like saying "I shall climb Mount Kilimanjaro to get a chocolate bar" - it's a very long way to go for chocolate, and you're probably not going to find chocolate there anyway. The convent won't wash away your hot temper. Trying to keep your perfect life perfect will stress you out. Even after losing x pounds, you'll still feel very self-conscious in your sexy get up.

If you want to be happier, what would make you feel happier today?

If you want to be sexier, what would make you feel sexier today?

If you want to be free, what would make you feel freer today?

If you want to be powerful, what would make you feel powerful today?

I know this is the opposite of what we've been taught all these years - that to feel a certain way, you have to achieve a certain goal, but **conventional wisdom has it backwards, and always has**. This thinking creates an endless chase – to be happy, you need the right job, relationship, car, cushions. Then you get them, and you're still not happy, so what do you chase next?

Step out of the wacky race that you can never win, and start to be who and how you want to be. Be who you want to be first, then go for the things you want. It might change what you go for because you won't be chasing a will'o the wisp anymore, but who cares when you get to be powerful, sexy, happy, calm, free, joyful today?

Be nice to the mirror

When you look in the mirror, what do you see? What do you say? Is it a constant litany of "you looked tired, you have more wrinkles, stop scowling misery guts and oh my god is that a GREY HAIR?" Or do you look in the mirror and say "hi gorgeous, you look absolutely stunning today".

Most of us spend our time with the mirror reinforcing every mean thought we ever had about ourselves. That's so mean to that poor mirror (not to mention the beautiful, sensitive, clever soul looking back at you). Get into the habit of saying something nice every time you look in the mirror - even just "hi sweetheart" is better than "look at that fat backside".

Imagine that woman you see in the mirror is the person you adore most in the world. You know she's not perfect, but she's sweet and kind and loving and she is trying really hard to be a good person, and she needs your support. She needs you to help her be the best her she can be (and calling her a fat, old cow isn't going to cut the mustard).

Imagine that every word you say to that beautiful woman in the mirror cuts straight to her heart and either breaks it a little bit or fills it with love. Imagine that the words you say to her make a difference to how good or bad she feels about herself. They do. So take care with what you say to the mirror – think about it, think about what impact your words will have.

Think about the impact you want to have on the woman in the mirror. Do you want her to have the best life possible for her? Do you want her to feel amazing about herself? Do you want her to walk out of the door feeling sexy, confident and full of joie de vivre? If so, make sure what you're saying to the mirror helps that vision, not hinders it.

What you see in the mirror is a reflection of how you see yourself, not a reflection of who you really are. When you change what you say to yourself in the mirror, you start to change what you see too. A client of mine used her mirror to beat herself up for being overweight, old, and ugly. It was impossible for her to say she was slim, young and beautiful because she didn't think it was true.

What she could say was that she had great boobs, she looked young for her age (in her words "I'm not 19 anymore, but I don't look 47") and she had beautiful eyes. That was enough for her to start seeing herself in a better light, and seeing that although she didn't look 19 anymore (being 47), she did look great for her age. The nicer she was to her mirror, the nicer the mirror was to her, until a friend asked if she'd had a facelift because she looked younger.

I can't guarantee friends will suspect you of closet plastic surgeries, but I can tell you that when you are nice to the mirror, the mirror responds (it works the other way too, but that's no fun). Tell the mirror the good things you want to hear, and that you can believe, and use the mirror to build yourself up instead of tearing yourself down.

Forgive yourself

Ok, listen. I know that you have messed up in your life. Who hasn't? Life is sometimes messy, and we fail and fall, and hurt people and make a fool of ourselves on a fairly regular basis. All of us do. Even those really cool people you see on TV/in your street/in your company, they have all messed up somehow.

Most of the time we do it accidentally, but sometimes we are deliberately malicious and vile. You have to forgive yourself anyway. You are always doing the best you can. Most of us don't set out to be a jackass, it just happens. We make mistakes *because we're human*.

I know that sucks – I would prefer to be a robot too. Er, no, wait, I don't want to be a robot at all. Ok, I would prefer to be perfect. No, wait, have you seen Stepford Wives? That's some creepy shit. I don't want to be perfect either. Ok, so it just sucks. Being human, being a real boy, being a human is to be flawed, and imperfect and, frankly, weird (which is a Very Good Thing in my book).

Then we have to interact with other flawed, imperfect, weird humans, and chaos can ensue. Then after the fact, we get to judge ourselves with Eagle Eye Hindsight. Yeah, it's so easy to see what you should have done once it's all over, but at the time, you're just doing your best with the circumstances and resources you have then. If you went back with the same knowledge and the same sequence of events, you'd probably do it the same way. Next time maybe you'll do it better/differently.

Sometimes you get it wrong. Forgive yourself. Not doing so doesn't make you a better person, it makes you under confident and fearful. One of the most memorable moments in my life was when I forgave my younger self for being so shy and quiet. She felt she had been in the wrong all this time.

My younger self was brave and strong and awesome but because (at the time) I thought I was wrong, I had to forgive myself for it 20+ years later. It still brings tears to my eyes that the teenage me felt so defective that she needed forgiveness and I have vowed never to make any part of me feel like that again.

So forgive yourself. For whatever wrongs you've done. You were doing the best you could at the time. We all are. Forgive yourself, vow to do better next time or to never do that again if you need to, and move on. Carrying around guilt and shame for whatever real or imagined wrongs you've done doesn't help you or the people you may have hurt. It just hurts you, so learn to forgive yourself.

Take *EXCELLENT* care of yourself

Ok, I could talk about this one for hours. So much so, I'm writing a book about it (due out late 2019). The crux of it is this: when you are not taking care of yourself, life is harder. When you are not taking great care of yourself, you don't feel as good. It's an absolute no-brainer that most people inexplicably ignore.

Want to feel good? Want life to be easier? Want to have more confidence? Want to have a healthy body? Want to have a healthy mind? Want to have a healthy heart (emotionally and physically)? Want to have a healthy spirit? Take care of yourself then.

There are so many objections to self-care, so let's take care of a couple of the most common ones here and now.

Self-care is selfish.

WRONG.

It is not even remotely selfish to make sure that you are running at your very best in all ways – this overflows onto everyone else in your life and you have more to give. It is more selfish to NOT take care of yourself because you are depleted, fed up and eventually you get sick.

Self-care takes too much time and I'm too busy.

WRONG.

You don't need to take hours and hours for your self-care. You can start caring for yourself more with just a few minutes a day. This excuse stops us from even trying to make changes, and it's just not true. You can take care of yourself in whatever time you have, you can make self-care part of your day (dance party while cooking dinner for example) and if you're busy, you need more self-care, not less.

"I have so much to do today, I better meditate twice as long" – Dalai Lama

Someone else should take care of my self-care.

WRONG.

I hear this one from clients a lot. Listen, I'm all for delegating, but when it comes to YOUR self-care, YOU need to take charge. Other people have no idea what you need from them – often we have no idea ourselves what we need from others. Don't give your power away to someone else on this one. It's a lovely idea, but it means putting unfair pressure on others to do something that only you can really do.

Excellent self-care of your body, mind, heart and soul will improve your life. So start taking better care of yourself right now.

Try this exercise with me: put your hand over your heart, take 3 deep breaths into your heart, and ask your heart "How cared for do I feel right now on a scale of 1-10, where 1 is 'I don't' and 10 is 'cradled in the arms of love'?" Let your heart answer – your head will try to butt in and argue it should be higher or lower, let your heart answer.

Whether your number is a 2 or an 8, your mission is to move it up one. From 2 to 3; from 5 to 6; from 8 to 9. You can again ask your heart what you could do today to move it up just one point. Don't make it complicated and try to do 5 hours meditation, 7 hours yoga and spend 28 hours with your best friend. Your heart will usually tell you something you CAN do, you just may need to throw out a few misconceptions about how it should be done.

For example, you can meditate for 1 minute. It's not ideal, but it is fine if that's all the time you have. It doesn't take a fortune to take great care of yourself either – a lot of the basic self-care things I do for myself cost nothing at all. Whatever level of income you are on, take the best care of yourself you can.

If you need some more help with what to do for self-care, get over to donnaonthebeach.com where you'll find lots of articles to help you take care of you. If your self-care is less than a 10 right now, I cannot recommend highly enough that you do so.

Own your quirks and weirdities

"You did not come here to be normal, you came here to be you." Robert Holden

We all have our little quirks and weirdnesses. We're all eccentric in our own ways. I often say that I don't know one person who isn't barmy in their own special way, and I mean it as a compliment. I'm not talking about poor mental health, I'm talking about those idiosyncrasies and foibles that make a person uniquely them and uniquely weird.

Now, let me just say now I'm talking good weird – unique, individual, not *normal*. I'm not talking here about the bad weird – stalkerish and creepy. You don't want to be that - it'll get you arrested eventually and freak people out. The good weird – that's what you want to be. Because there is no such thing as an average person. We're all as different as can be.

And we all have our own little quirks and weirdities. Over the years, I've had so many conversations with people about very random stuff – and found other people with the same quirks as me. That 'oh my god, **me too**!' moment that is so delightful when you realise you're not the only person in the world who doesn't like cold tomato.

Room temperature and cooked tomatoes are fine – fresh from the fridge – euw, makes my teeth ache. When I found that someone else I knew felt the same I realised it was not just totally batty and weird – someone else agreed with me. I don't know why that feels better, but it does.

The same with all my other little quirks – I don't like butter or margarine that looks like it's been savaged by bears – use it neatly or stay out of my butter. I have to have money in my purse neatly with the Queen's heads together – it makes me twitch when people have higgledy-piggledy money (and I have been known to sort all the money in a till so it all faces the right way).

We all have our funny little habits and mannerisms. Own them. Embrace them. If you're tipping over the edge into OCD and those funny habits are getting in the way of you living your life, then get help. For most of us, our idiosyncrasies are just a part of who we are. A part that all too often gets dismissed and disowned, because no one likes to be seen as a weirdo.

Everyone is weird to some degree. Everyone I know has some oddity about them – it's what makes us who we are. Our unique collection of personality traits plus experience plus habits plus environment makes us all different from one another. This is as it should be.

There is no such thing as a *normal* person. If we were all the same, it would be a very boring world. The quirks and idiosyncrasies and weirdnesses of my friends are what I love most about them. As much as we didn't want to be the eccentric old biddies we knew as kids, now I'm willing to bet that they were the happiest people of all.

Instead of being constrained by the strait-jacket of normality, they were themselves – odd quirks, eccentric dress sense, their own shade of weird. They just didn't give a rat's ass if people who didn't know them thought they were weird.

"It's weird not to be weird" – John Lennon

I suspect that most of the people who ever created anything, who ever invented anything, who ever did anything different, were weird. They had to be to do things against the norm. So think of your heroes of music, science, literature, exploration and follow their weird example by owning your quirks and idiosyncrasies.

Fall in love with yourself

You? You're AWESOME. The very best you there ever was. What's not to love? I know that you have a thousand examples of how you're not awesome. I know that you know all your character defects intimately and that you remember every incident where you messed up or made a fool of yourself. (At the same time you conveniently forget all your wonderful characteristics and all the times you got it right.)

It's hard to fall in love with yourself when you know how flawed and imperfect you are. Let me rephrase that: it's hard to fall in love with yourself when you only concentrate on those flaws and imperfections, and when you only see them as bad. Many of your bad characteristics have positive interpretations too, and you can learn to love your shyness, your stubbornness, your impatience.

I didn't love my shyness until someone else pointed out the beauty of shy, the vulnerability of it, and the strength in shy. There are many other characteristics I didn't love until I learned to love them. Stubbornness and bloody-mindedness make me very persistent, a trait I needed to keep my business going for over a decade. Impatience makes me more likely to take action. My sharp tongue exercises my wit.

I could keep going. There are some traits I'm still looking for the positive spin on and finding a way to love – short-temperedness and general irritability being one. I don't suffer fools gladly, that's the only plus I can come up with. I do accept that I am short-tempered and irritable at times – it helps me to manage my self-care because if I don't take care of myself, I'm like a bear with a sore backside.

All of the things I've made a mess of, I learned from. They've shaped my character, made me who I am. I love and accept myself anyway. You need to too. You're going to have to put up with yourself your whole life, so you might as well find a way to fall head over heels with the weird and wonderful individual that is you.

There's not another one of you in the whole world. You're unique and special and you deserve to have the love and backing of yourself. Like many of the ideas in this book, this is a definite process – I didn't love myself at all, and then I learned to over many years. I learned to notice the good things about me. I learned to reframe the bad stuff and see the light aspect of a characteristic that's seen as defective or deficient.

So start the process here. Learn to fall in love with you. Beautiful, unique, special, wonderful you.

Live by YOUR values

We all have things that are important to us – maybe freedom, joy, honesty, challenge, creativity, love, kindness, ambition - the values that are important to us. They're different for each person and they have a huge impact on how we live our lives. Yet many of us don't even know what our most important values are.

When we don't know what's truly important to us, we can't understand why we keep rubbing up against the same problems, or why we do the things we do; or why we feel so uncomfortable in certain situations or with certain people. Once I worked out my top values, I could see why I was bouncing off the walls of every job I ever had, because my top value was freedom.

This value is at the heart of my Vision Statement "to have the freedom to follow my inspiration every day, wherever it may lead". You might guess that inspiration is also in my top 5. Others that are important to me include joy, honesty, individuality, open-mindedness and learning.

This explains why I go back to the cashier to tell them they've undercharged me (to the bafflement of other customers and usually the cashier themselves). I'm honest. I don't even think about it, I just do it. It's one of my top values. My values explain why I chose a career that I enjoy, that gives me the freedom to work how I want, in which I am constantly learning and growing.

Your values will give you similar clues about why you do what you do, and why you struggle with certain situations – like working for a rigid boss in a boring job with no fun. Meh. It also helps you figure out how you can express those values and enjoy them right now. Whatever your current circumstances, you can always find ways to express and live to what's important to you.

Even if you currently feel trapped in a job you don't enjoy, if you know you have strong values of freedom and joy you can remind yourself how free you are – free to say what you want, believe what you want, wear what you want. You can ensure that even if your work life isn't joyous, you can shoehorn joy into your life in other areas, and you can set yourself a challenge of bringing joy into the office.

You can start to let go of those things, situations and people who conflict with your values and stop living by other people's values. Parents, friends, society at large all influence our perception of what's right; but until you know what is truly important to YOU, you can't honour those values in your life. Knowing your values is like having the master password to your best life because anything that brings you closer to what's most important to you will bring you closer to loving your life.

To get the exercise I use with my clients to find their top values, go to donnaonthebeach.com/blog/freebies/values-exercise.

Once you've figured out what's really important to you in your life, you can start to live to those values. You can make sure that your life is about the things that are most important to you, not just about getting through one day after another with no adventure or fun or love or dignity or justice or whatever matters most to you.

Own your magnificence

I want you to think for a moment about your best friend. Imagine him or her radiating warmth, effervescence, joy and delight. Imagine them glittering, incandescently shining with brilliance. Showing the world that they are a sparkling example of the stunning beauty of the human soul.

Imagine them seeing themselves through your eyes, as you see them. As the kindest, funniest, most intelligent, most loving, most brilliant person you know. Imagine them really owning how flipping great they are. Imagine them being their very best selves all the time – imagine them as healthy, happy, strong and powerful and living the life they dream of deep down in their heart.

Now imagine yourself in the same way. Imagine every wonderful thing about you being fully shown, instead of hidden away. Imagine really owning your magnificence. Really owning it – seeing yourself in the way the people who love you the most see you. As beautiful and fun and lovely and clever and witty and capable and wondrous.

Maybe you already feel that. Maybe you already know how great you are, and you don't hide any of your brilliance. If so, congratulations – keep shining. However if like so many of us, you do not fully own how amazing you are, it's time to start getting it. You are incredible. You have such wonderful gifts and talents, even if you don't know what they are yet.

Trust me, they're there. You are a shining light. You have an inner radiance that is incandescent and stunningly beautiful. We all do. Unfortunately, that light gets covered up with all sorts of rubbish. Imagine a diamond that has been covered up over the years in nonsense about not being good enough, in criticism, in fear, in bullshit about being perfect, in stress.

The diamond is still there, and occasionally, when you are at your best, it shines through and dazzles the people around you. Your mission, should you choose to accept it, is to clean the debris off the diamond so it can shine more and more fully – so you can shine more and more fully. You can approach this in two ways – one, shine so brightly that you burn the debris off from inside; and two, clear off the debris – stop the habits and beliefs and fears that hide how fantastic you are and get rid of any lingering doubts and criticisms.

It's the work of a lifetime, but imagine if your best friend did it. Imagine them shining brightly, fully their magnificent selves, more and more wonderful each year, really understanding more and more how remarkable they are. Isn't that worth spending a few years doing?

"As we let our own light shine, we unconsciously give other people permission to do the same. As we are liberated from our own fear, our presence automatically liberates others." – Marianne Williamson

It starts with you. It starts with you recognising your brilliance, even if you only see a tiny bit of the wonder of you, that's a start. It continues with you opening up to shine and knowing that in doing so, your friends and family will bask in the warmth of your radiance. They will be encouraged to shine because you shine. The darkness in your world can be lit by your light and your love – will you rise to the challenge and begin to own your magnificence?

Believe in yourself

Let me ask you a question: if you believed in yourself 100%, what would you do differently? What dreams that have been shelved or ignored would you resurrect? What would you try? What would be different about your life?

I was an under-confident child – I was painfully shy, and had no self-belief and confidence, even though I was an intelligent child. The teachers who believed in me the most got the best out of me (even though they also terrified me). I didn't do the best in the subjects I felt I was good at, I did the best in the subjects where my teachers shored up my self-belief.

Luckily once I got out of school, I started to develop some self-confidence and belief in me - to the point that I went to the other side of the world on my own for a year, despite the fact I had never done anything remotely like that in my life. Now, I have a business in a profession I love, that barely a soul had heard of when I started, and I write books.

I believe in myself and my dreams so much that I follow them tenaciously. Even when it looks like I'm getting nowhere, I still keep going, because I believe in me and in my dreams. Without that level of self-belief, I would never even have acknowledged my dream to write, never mind actually written anything.

Without that self-belief, I would not have written another book after my first one bombed. Without that self-belief, I would still be feeling trapped in a life that stifled my soul. Self-belief is the reason you're reading this. I'm not all the way there. I haven't got a completely unshakable 100% level of self-belief yet. The amount of self-belief I do have has led me down paths I would never have dreamed of.

If you had told me a year before I went travelling in Australia that I would have travelled to the other side of the world on my own, I'd have had you locked up. If you had told me when I was 14 that 2 years later I'd be working in a pub, and full of self-confidence, I'd have assumed you had the wrong person. If you had told me when I was 17 that I'd write a book (and have 7 that I plan to write) I'd have laughed in your face.

So those things you don't yet believe you can do? You can. You need to start believing in you. Or at least in the possibility that you could maybe do it. You can get cheerleaders and coaches and supporters (I did) to shore up your self-belief when you need to, but ultimately, you're the one with the keys to your life. You're the one who needs to believe in you enough to take the action and make the changes and hire the help you need to make your dreams a reality.

You're the one who needs to believe that you are more capable than you realise, that your dreams are more reachable than you fear, that you have gifts and talents and resources that will get you to wherever you need to go. You need to start believing in you. Like so many of the ideas in this book, it's a process, it's the work of years. I assure you, it is work worth doing.

How do you start believing in yourself? By taking steps in the faith that you'll figure it out. You can take big leaps of faith, you can also take baby steps of faith. You just take some action and trust that you'll figure out what to do next as you go along. Then you take some more action, and more and more until you're ready to take bigger risks because your self-belief is stronger.

Eventually, you will have a completely unshakable, 100% level of self-belief, and it will not even occur to you that you could fail.

Be your own Bezzie mate

Imagine for a moment having a friend who knows what you think before you can say it. Who takes one look at your face and knows exactly what mood you're in and what you need. Who believes in you so much that it brings tears to your eyes. Who loves you totally unconditionally, despite knowing all your flaws and faults and the bad things you've done.

Wouldn't that be amazing? To have this wonderful person in your corner all the time? Maybe you have some of this with your friends and partner, but the best person to fill this role is *you*. Our best friends and lovers might know us better than anyone else, but we still know ourselves even better than that. We might tell our coaches, partners and bezzie mates our deepest darkest fears and brightest most deeply held dreams, but we're the only ones who know them intimately.

Empathetic people can understand and feel for you, but they can't feel what you feel. You're the only one who's been through your whole life with you. You're the only one who's experienced every moment of your life. You are the best person to have as your best friend. You can't get rid of yourself, so you might as well be the best friend to yourself you can possibly be.

You can still have best friends and lovers and partners and people in your corner, but also be your own best friend. You're the one who knows you the best. You're the one who knows if you need a hug or to be left alone. You're the one who knows your deepest darkest secrets and deeply held big scary dreams.

You may have heard the saying "Everybody thought somebody should do it, nobody did". We leave the responsibility of being our best friend in the hands of our friends and family. The fact is no one else is going to get you like you do. No one else knows what we really need. Our best friends can do their best, and often they are spot on because they know us and love us.

But sometimes they miss the mark – often because we don't share our full truth, or we don't want to hurt them, or they don't want us to change and leave them. It is unrealistic and unfair to expect someone else to be everything to you. How can anyone else possibly know what you need, especially if you don't know? When you know you better than anyone.

I'm not talking about being a complete loner with no support system – I'm talking about having that great support system with fabulous friends and special spouses *and* being your own best friend. How? How would you treat your best friend in the whole wide world? Start there, by treating yourself the same way.

By respecting, loving and honouring yourself. By enjoying your own company. By being aware of your gifts and talents and brilliant quirks. By treating yourself. By taking an interest in your deepest desires. By listening to yourself. By encouraging you. By supporting your dreams. By sticking up for yourself when someone's doing you down. By being your own bezzie mate.

Don't reject any part of you

We all have different parts of ourselves, different sides to ourselves, pieces of our personality that we don't necessarily see as positive. Like the Gremlin, the inner critic, the ego, the victim, the saboteur, the protector-controller aspects of ourselves. A lot of current teaching focuses on taming those aspects, or getting rid of them, or ignoring them.

I subscribed to that view myself for a while – I agreed: just tell your inner critic to shut up. Then I started reading about the ego and how the ego was bad and we had to tame the ego or get rid of it, and I started to feel pretty uncomfortable with this view. Kick out the ego? Get rid of it? Really? Kill your inner gremlin? Lock up your inner critic? Hmm.

It's a part of you. This part that is *bad* is a part of you. So to me, this attitude of cutting it away, denying it, getting rid of it is kind of weird. You can't *get rid of it*. You can retrain that aspect of you and put it in its proper place. Not by locking it away but by seeking to understand it.

Every part of every body has a positive intention. The self-destructive part of you, the inner critic, the ego, all have a positive intention. They may not be fulfilling that intention, but they're doing the best they can. For me, the inner critic's positive intention is to motivate me. Honestly, I can't think of a worse way to motivate me.

I am not motivated by criticism – it's damaging, hurtful and actively de-motivating. But that's what my inner critic was trying to do. It's like a person put in a job with no training and no real job description – they do the best they can, but they're often quite ineffective (we've all worked with that person, right? Perhaps we've even been that person).

Once you find out what the positive intention is of your *bad* parts, you can retrain them, let them know what to do instead, and a better way of motivating you or keeping you safe, or helping you to enjoy your life. I had a client who was trying (without success) to get rid of their ego. I asked the positive intention of that ego and the answer was 'to help you have a great life'.

The way the ego was going about it was not helping. With a bit of retraining, that aspect of my client piped down and let their higher self take over the reins of the great life. Sometimes rather than needing to retrain, we just need to put the right part of us in the right job. The ego or protector/controller aspect takes over running our lives because no one else did.

I only discovered a few years ago that the creative, connected aspect of me needs to be in charge of my vision, and the inner doer is in charge of making it happen. That made life easier. Now, the inner creative comes up with the ideas, and the doer creates fun ways to keep on track and sit me at my desk (and loves creating spreadsheets and graphs to mark progress).

Put your inner child in charge of having fun in your life. Put your inner saboteur in charge of finding everything that might get in the way of you having an awesome life. Put your inner doer in charge of doing stuff (not dreaming up creative solutions, that's not its strength). Put your inner victim in charge of alerting you to when you're giving your power away to others or not taking care of yourself.

Don't demonise any part of you, because it's still part of you. It has a positive intention – and it either needs training or needs to be put in its right place. Not by rugby tackling it to the floor and tying it up, but by allowing each part of ourselves to play to our strengths. Once you do, it'll be a lot easier to love your life because you're not constantly fighting yourself and feeling like a split personality.

You are not a hippo, so stop wallowing

A hippo may love to wallow in mud but you, my dear, are not a hippo, and you do not need to wallow in things that are getting you down, situations that are annoying you, or relationship issues where someone is being an asshat.

It's ok to have a bit of a rant or process what's going on, but let it blow through like a refreshing breeze, not like covering yourself in mud and sitting in it. Shit happens. Let it go. I know that's easier said than done sometimes, and you just want to share and share and share the bad you've been done, but after a certain point, it stops helping.

Instead of feeling better after sharing, you feel worse, dirty, like you've been bathing in mud. You're just sitting in a muddy puddle of 'it's a terrible shame for me'. You notice that after sharing, your blood is boiling and you feel even more hard done by or let down or just plain fed up.

You are not a hippo - so quit wallowing. Process by all means, but if you're just wallowing in how terrible life is, get over it.

Many of us talk to each other to help us process what's happening in our lives, but instead of just having a rant and moving on, we're still talking about the same things months and years later. That's not processing, it's wallowing. If you've got into the habit of doing that, try a different way to process before you talk – like writing, dancing or exercising.

I always find that if I've done those things before I talk, I'm more clear about what I need to say, get help with, have witnessed, get rid of; and some of the sharpness of hurt, anger or fed-up-ness is dulled so I'm not quite so livid. It doesn't always work, and of course, there are situations in which it is not appropriate to pause the conversation to have a dance break.

If you find yourself wallowing, here's my favourite question to help you stop:

So, what are you going to do about it then?

Once you've had a chunter, or processed, or had a little bit of a rant, what are you going to do about it now? How are you going to change it? Because moaning and wallowing in your misery is no fun and doesn't tend to change anything. So, what you gonna do 'bout it?

"Where there's no wood, the fire goes out; and where there is no talebearer, strife ceases" Proverbs 26:20

It's not often I quote the bible, but this is so apt. If you keep feeding the fire of whatever is getting on your wick or getting you down, the fire will continue to burn. If you step out of the mud and stop wallowing, the strife you are causing yourself will cease. The outer circumstance may not change, but you won't be covering yourself in mud, which can only be a good thing.

P.S. I am not talking here about deep-seated problems, I'm talking about day to day things that get on your nerves and can be easily let go.

Don't judge yourself so harshly

I know that you want to be the best you that you can be. I know that you want to do your very best at whatever you do. I know you want to love your life and make your dreams come true. I know you want to be happy. I know you think that if you get it *right*, you will be happy.

There's a teeny, tiny problem with this desire though. In order to be our best, do our best and get it right, we have a tendency to push ourselves and judge ourselves harshly. Anything less than perfection is met with a litany of self-judgement. Too often we examine our performance and find ourselves wanting.

It's one of the top things I work on with my clients because they all do it. They're all really hard on themselves. I recognise it because I am too. I wouldn't care about it if it worked. If it helped them be the best, do their best, love their life, make their dreams come true and be happy, I'd say 'hey, go judge yourself harshly, it's really working for you'.

It doesn't work. It actively undermines us. Being hard on ourselves and judging ourselves harshly erodes our self-esteem, saps our confidence and hurts us. This does not help us to do better, be better or be happy. It makes us fearful of our own judgement, uneasy and hesitant. It's not easy to take action, or just to live your life, in fear of the barrage of criticism that comes your way when you fall short of your own unrealistic expectations.

Judging yourself harshly leads to more unhelpful behaviour – beating yourself up (self-criticism), guilt, shame, even making you angry with yourself. This genuinely isn't the best way to get the best from yourself. In fact, for many of us, it's the worst way to try to get the best from ourselves. I was telling a client that I am a bit of a mardy teenager, so when people criticise me (including me), I tend to rebel, to act out, to turn my back on whatever they're trying to get me to do.

I could hear the penny dropping for him over the phone – he (like me) hated working for people he could never please. He found it so demotivating to be criticised and condemned for every little thing he did wrong. Yet when he became self-employed, he did the same thing to himself and then wondered why it didn't work.

Funny, isn't it? We all seem to do it though. So can you imagine dropping the judgement of yourself? You can still notice what's not working, just without the additional commentary of 'you suck'. One of my clients had been beating herself up for spending hours messing about on Facebook instead of working on her dream. Once we dropped the judgement, she realised she went to Facebook when she felt stuck.

Once she found this out, she could try other ways of getting unstuck – like dance breaks, writing about it, meditation, talking it out with her hubby. While she was busy kicking her own behind about it, there was no room for insight and wisdom. The problem is very rarely that you are stupid and lazy. It's usually something else, but if you spend your time judging yourself harshly, you'll never find out what the true problem is.

If that problem is low self-confidence, judging yourself harshly is just going to make it worse and worse. So drop the gavel, take off the silly wig and stop judging yourself so harshly. You are doing your best, and if that isn't working for you, figure out why, given that you are fabulous and committed. What's getting in the way? You can't discover what that is if you're too busy beating yourself up.

You're never too old

"You are never too old to set another goal or dream a new dream" – C.S Lewis

In some cultures, age is perceived as a good thing. The older you are, the wiser you are, the more experience you have of life, the more your journey is etched into your face; and this is a good thing. We have a particularly youth-obsessed culture – people spend thousands on looking odd, I mean, on looking younger.

Trout pouts, foreheads that don't move, strange stretched faces. If that's your thing, I'm not criticising it. I wouldn't do it – largely because I don't want people to wonder if I'm livid, I want them to see it in my face. One side effect of this youth-obsessed culture is that there's a perception that old is bad. Once you're old, you're past it, your life is over, you're a has-been.

When I was under 30, I thought 30 was old. I thought that anything I hadn't done by the time I was 30 wouldn't get done because I'd then be *too old*. Thankfully, I was every shade of wrong. When I was under 30, I thought turning 30 would be the Worst Thing Ever. It wasn't. Actually, once I got past 30, I started to chill out, settle into my life, accept and love myself, and realise that everything I thought about age was nonsense.

40 is ancient? Balderdash. You can't do anything worthwhile after 30? Absurd. It's all downhill from 30 on? Poppycock. In my experience, life has got better every year. In my 20's I was miserable, stressed out, almost frantic to *have an amazing life*. In my 40's I'm enjoying life. I don't really care if it's amazing or not. As long as I enjoy it, it doesn't need to be headline-making and earth-shattering.

Anyway, back to the main point. You're never too old. You're never too old to do things you want to do. You're never too old to fall in love with your life. Even if you've been hacked off with life for the last 20/40/60 years, it's never too late to make a change. When you're dead, it's too late. Before that point, it's not.

If you've got time left, you've got time to do stuff. It's not too late. Ok, maybe you can't play football for England if you're 56, or become an ice dancer at 42, or be the under 18 world champion gymnast at 29. Still, you could play football, dance on ice, or play about on gym equipment at any age. There may be some dreams you had once that you genuinely can't do now, but there aren't many.

A few years ago, I came across the wonderful Daryn Kagan's blog. Daryn was a CNN news anchor whose contract wasn't renewed, so she created a website dedicated to showing the world what's possible. One of the categories was 'over 60', and it was super inspiring. 80-year-olds who got college degrees, 90-year-old marathon runners, granny drummers, an 89-year-old who just learned to read.

If you think it's too late for you to do anything at all because you're too old, I encourage you to look for stories of later life inspiration. You won't think you're too old for long. Another fabulous inspiration is Louise Hay, who wrote her first book at 50 and started a publishing company at 58. She died at age 90, having written over 20 books and inspired millions of people.

Still think you're too old? You don't have to write or drum or start a publishing company – you just have to live the life YOU want to live. Now. Not tomorrow or in the next life. Now. It's never too late. As the 89-year-old who learned to read said: "You're not going to learn in that pine box" – so go now and do some stuff you want to do. Because whatever age you are, that's the perfect age for you to do what you want to do.

Ditch perfectionism

Nobody's perfect, not even me. Perfection is just too much like hard work – trying to do the impossible is hard. This does not mean you now become indolent and lazy and rubbish at everything you do. It means you do your best, knowing that perfection doesn't exist.

10 seconds after you've dusted and polished, a speck of dust will fall on your perfectly dusted table. The book you think is finished - you'll think of a new chapter for or find a spilling moostick an hour later (I know). The perfectly crafted façade of supermom will fall off when your alarm fails to go off and you're taking the kids to school in your pyjamas (so I've heard).

There is nothing wrong with wanting to be the best you that you can be. But guess what? Perfectionism doesn't help you achieve that. It actually hinders it. It undermines your confidence, makes you nit-pick about things no one else would notice, makes you question yourself, procrastinate, and never finish anything, because it's never perfect.

This book (you may have noticed) is not perfect. It has flaws. There's probably a spelling mistake I've missed. The drawings are, well, um, how do I put it? They're not perfect. Some of them aren't even right good. I redid the terrible ones because I wasn't happy with them, but the rest I've left.

I could (easily) have waited until I had more experience and was better at drawing stick figures, but then you wouldn't be reading this book. Or it wouldn't have silly drawings in it. They're good enough. Hopefully your inner art critic isn't cringing with distaste or revulsion, and more importantly, hopefully, a couple of them have amused you and helped me make my point. (Honestly, even if you haven't enjoyed them, they've made me laugh aloud, so it's all good.)

We say 'I'm a perfectionist' like it's a good thing. It's not. It makes you critical, you set unrealistically high standards, and you get annoyed when things aren't perfect, which is all the time. So you're always annoyed. That's no fun. It's not necessary either. Good enough will do.

You don't have to settle for mediocrity, you can strive for excellence – just not perfection. Perfection is an illusion, a dangerous illusion that will make you bloody miserable. So let yourself be good enough. Let what you do be good enough. Let other people's efforts be good enough. Ditch the perfectionism and enjoy your life instead.

Part 5:

Sleep, crying,

enthusiasm and

passion

Sleep

Who can fall in love with life when they're tired? Who can fall in love with life if they're constantly dragging their sorry, exhausted ass through life? You need to get enough sleep for you, whether that's 10 hours a night or 4. Never mind if what's right for Mr Average is 6 hours or 7 hours or whatever it is. What is right for *you*?

I am a bit of a sleep Tyrant. I love sleep, always have, and was often considered lazy as a child. However, if I don't get enough sleep, I am tired. If I'm tired, I'm a misery-guts. If I'm a misery-guts, I'm not loving life. Plus, if I don't get enough sleep for a few days in a row, I turn from a mild-mannered cheery lovely lady to a psychotic homicidal bitch from hell. So sleep is not just a nice idea, it's a health and safety issue (everyone else's health and safety specifically).

If you're constantly tired, go to bed a little early. If you get more sleep and are less tired, you'll be able to get more done in the hours you're awake, making up for the extra time asleep. Sleep helps us physically, mentally and emotionally – it makes us feel better in a hundred different ways. Never mind all the Type A bullshit sayings "sleeping's cheating" etc. – get enough sleep, and get good quality sleep.

There's lots of stuff you can try to help you sleep better (as a 20+ year insomniac, I have tried many of them) – find your magic formula for plenty of lovely sleep. Because, if you're not constantly exhausted and using matchsticks to hold your eyes open, you can more easily fall in love with life.

Cry when you need to

Emotion is normal. Holding it in creates a messy head and a hurty heart. Most of us have been trained not to cry, not to show emotion, or weakness, but that doesn't mean we don't feel it. Just because you keep the tears inside, that doesn't make it hurt less. In fact, I have a theory that it actually hurts more.

A University of South Florida study suggested 88.8% of people felt better after a good cry. (I love that description – have a good cry rather than a bad cry or maybe a messy cry or a deranged cry. Anyway.) Crying (for most of us) makes us feel better – that's because it's a release.

Like laughing, or exercise, or dancing, or shouting, or primal screaming, crying is a release mechanism. So if we don't cry because we're big, brave and strong, what we're doing is holding in the hurt and the emotion. At some point, that's going to come flying out in another direction.

Or it'll stay inside, rotting and poisoning your body, hardening your heart. I know that sounds a bit melodramatic, but I whole-heartedly believe that pent up emotion is really bad for you. So cry when you need to. I know you cannot just cry whenever you want – it's not appropriate in a job interview for example, or during sex (see Grey's Anatomy Season 2 episodes 18 & 19).

Most of us prefer to be alone and at home to have a good cry. So you may have to wait a little while. Just don't bottle it up forever. Give yourself some weepy time. I am fortunate, I cry quite easily - at adverts, if animals die in films, while watching great sporting achievement; and if I have PMT, I will cry at anything at all.

Sometimes I cannot cry when I feel the need, so I stopper it up a bit, then pull out the "Beaches" DVD, or a sad song or two. I used to have a crying playlist, then I realised I was using it to wallow, so I stopped, but I can always think of a song or three that'll set me off if I need it.

When my uncle died, I cried. I cried at the funeral. I cried a few times with family. But it was only when I was alone and I howled and wailed and sobbed that I started to feel the cathartic effect of crying. Sometimes a little weep into a handkerchief is just not enough to release the emotion.

Releasing the grief and pain and hurt and sorrow from your heart allows your heart to begin to heal. Letting go of the emotions built up by everyday life allows you to feel lighter and release some of the burdens. If you are holding onto emotion, let it go (and of course, if you need support while you're doing so, get it).

Sort out your energy levels

If having MS has taught me anything (other than how to survive an MRI if you're claustrophobic – wear an eye mask), it's that I have to manage my energy. I have to refuel. I am not the energiser bunny. I'm not superhuman. As much as I would like to just go from activity to activity, from social engagement to social engagement, from client to client, from task to task, I cannot.

If I try, I burn out. I don't enjoy half the things I do, because I'm too busy running on adrenalin. My attention is scattered, my mood is lowered, and I'm just bloody worn out. When I first started to get fatigue (which is not just tired, by the way, asshat doctor who told me to get more sleep when I was getting 12 hours a night at 27 years of age), I fought it like a tiger.

I wanted my life back. I wanted to work and go out and burn the candle from both ends and in the middle. I wanted to be energetic and lively and the life and soul of the party. I wanted to just keep doing and doing and doing. Even writing that is making me feel tired now. Fortunately for me, my body was having none of it. The more I tried to fight the fatigue, the more exhausted I got.

The less I managed my energy, the more my energy levels kicked my feet out from under me and landed me on my rump. The more I fought, the more I lost. It took me a while to pay attention. Years, in fact. Eventually, I got it, my energy is not an inexhaustible resource that will keep me powered up forever without any refuelling.

Duh. No shit, Sherlock, right? Still, most of us seem to think that refuelling is for wimps. Imagine if you treated your car that way? "Whaddaya mean, you have no fuel? Come on you great sissy, keep driving." Your car would just stop. It's not selfish, it's not a feeble namby-pamby wimp; it just has no fuel. Without fuel, it will not work. Simple. It's not self-indulgent; it's just out of fuel.

Humans apparently don't need to refuel. Ever. Or if they do, 5 hours sleep and a cereal bar will do it. Hmm. I don't think so. When you really think about it for more than a second, you'll see (as I did, after a few years of fighting it) that this is beyond ridiculous, and with that attitude, no wonder half the world is always exhausted.

Try this exercise with me: put your hand over your heart, take 3 deep breaths into your heart, and ask your heart "How energised am I feeling right now on a scale of 1-10, where 1 is 'I could lie face down on the floor and be very happy to stay there' and 10 is 'I AM LIKE TIGGER! BOUNCE! BOUNCE!'?" Let your heart answer – your head will try to butt in and argue it should be higher or lower, but let your heart answer.

Whether your number is a 2 or an 8, your mission is to move it up one. From 2 to 3; from 5 to 6; from 8 to 9. You can again ask your heart what you could do today to move your energy level up just one point. Let your heart answer, not your head. Your heart will come up with something gentle and easy (your head will normally want to put that idea on steroids).

Don't make it complicated and try to fill the tank to overflowing first go. It's that obsession with doing it all NOW that got us all into energetic trouble in the first place. Just move it up a point at a time until you are a beautiful blend of Tigger and Zebedee and you're absolutely full of bounce and energy.

Get fresh air

Get outside and let the beauty of nature revive your spirit. Like your momma always said, fresh air IS good for you. Nature is good for you. Find a place nearby that is beautiful and open and enjoy it as often as you can, or just get out of your house and walk to the shop now and again.

I know it's easier to just get in the car, but your legs are useful. Use them. Smell the roses, hear the birds, feel the sun (or the rain, or the wind, or even the snow) on your face, breathe the air, see the beauty that nature has to offer.

Nature is soothing, outside air has a fresh quality, and being outdoors seems to blow away the cobwebs and give you back perspective. Being outside also gives you a chance for reflective, calm time in a world that seems to have no off switch. Nature, fresh air, the great outdoors give you a chance to at least press pause, if not stop.

Instead of constantly being bombarded by information and non-stop doing, you can go outside to walk; to stare at the stars; to listen to the wind in the branches; to watch the sun rise or set; to feel the sun on your face; to dance in the rain; or just to let your mind settle down. Getting outside is fabulous self-care – it is good for us physically, mentally, emotionally and spiritually.

I know, you don't want to when it's cold, it's raining, it's dark, it's horrible. Without the dog with her hopeful looks at me from the moment I get up, I wouldn't leave the house in winter unless I absolutely had to. Thanks to the dog, I know it will be worth it – I always feel better when I've been outside for some fresh air. Even in the depths of winter or when it's peeing down with rain, I feel better with some oxygen and countryside time.

You don't have to hike over fell and dale, you can just find a local park to enjoy on a regular basis, and somewhere special you can go to when you have time. Wherever you feel called to - the seaside, the forest, the mountains, the countryside - go there. Let nature soothe your spirit. Let fresh air fill your lungs. Let the modern world go, just for a little while and enjoy air that is fresh and the feel of the sun on your face.

Believe with all your heart

What do you believe in? Do you believe in God? In Goddesses? In angels? In a benevolent universe? In possibility? In dreams coming true? Whatever you believe in, believe in it with all your heart. Let it be a big part of your life if you want it to be. Don't try to be cool and cynical if you're not. Live by your own philosophy.

I believe in a benevolent universe. I believe in a loving God or Goddess – in a Divine spirit of some sort. I believe in Angels. I believe in miracles. I believe in the basic goodness of the human being. I believe animals should be treated well and that people who mistreat their pets will suffer in pet heaven, where they will be bitten, chased, kicked, trodden on, starved and beaten by the Karma cats and dogs.

I believe in Heaven. I don't think people play harps there though (unless they want to). I believe in souls. I believe in Divine Inspiration. I believe that the purpose of life is to enjoy it (without harming others). I believe all of this with all my heart, and it makes me happy.

I don't need you to believe in any of it. I don't care if your concept of the Divine is different from mine. Just as I don't care if your concept of what constitutes good music matches mine. It's my beliefs, they're my business. Yours are your business. If you believe in nothing you cannot see and touch, that's your business.

But if you believe in weird and wonderful stuff, believe it with your whole heart – embrace it in your life and live as if you live in a miraculous and wonderful universe where anything is possible. It is tempting in some places to believe what your neighbours believe – whether they are Jesus' sunbeams or atheists, but your beliefs are your business.

It's your life. So believe what you believe with your whole heart, and give others the respect to do the same – if they believe in fairies and unicorns and a vengeful God, that's their business. (By the way, I'm open minded on the idea of fairies and unicorns, but the vengeful God thing, that's just not the Divine Spirit I believe in.)

Have enthusiasm for your life

Cool is *so* last year darling. Get EXCITED. If you're going to do something, do it with your whole heart, don't be half-assed about your life. Get enthusiastic about your life and everything in it. Get enthusiastic about everything you have planned, from lunch with a friend to a holiday by the sea.

Get enthusiastic about daily things - your favourite TV show, bath time, reading your favourite book, enjoying a walk in the park at lunchtime, eating your favourite sandwich. If you're thinking "that sounds silly and childish", YES. Who says kids get the monopoly on over the top enthusiasm?

Take an interest in your life, even if you think it's not interesting enough. If you spend your whole life being bored and uninterested in anything, it will be boring. If you take an interest and get enthused about your life, it will be interesting and fun and fabulous.

You don't have to be a jet-setting, superstar-clubbing, tabloid-headlining person to have an interesting, fun and fabulous life. (In fact, that whirlwind life is my idea of hell.) This is your life – what's interesting to you? Get enthused about that. What do you find fun? Get enthused about that. What is your idea of fabulous? That's what you need to be enthusiastic about.

Whether you're a geek or a party animal, an introvert or an extrovert, a cool kid or a total nerd, get enthused about what YOU find appealing. I used to be a big clubber. Nowadays, I'm far more enthusiastic about a new book than a big night out. That's fine – it's my life, I get to be enthusiastic about music and books and Stargazing Live; and anything else my geeky introverted heart loves.

Get enthusiastic about what you've got in your life right now. Being blasé and indifferent about your life is depressing. Especially when there are things worth getting enthusiastic about – there are things worth taking a moment to 'woohoo' about. Don't leave enthusiasm for only the big, obvious, life-changing things; be enthusiastic about the small, the curious, the things that make up your life.

What can you get enthusiastic about today? Have you got a TV show you are looking forward to watching, a catch up with a friend to look forward to, a bag of crisps? Hey, no judgement here, I am saying get enthusiastic about it all – participate in your life fully, with energy and zeal. Why? Because it's easy to love a life you're eager to be part of. It's hard to love a life you're apathetic about.

Let your passions play a part in your life

What are you passionate about? What gets you standing on your soapbox, waving your arms in the air? What could you do for hours and hours without ceasing? What excites and inspires you? What makes you come alive? What do you do even when you have no time or money for it? What do you miss doing? What do you wish you could do?

Your passions don't have to be cool or huge, world-saving passions. You could have a passion for stamps or chess or books or technical stuff or music or plants or knitting or museums or history or furniture. Whatever. They're your passions - indulge them, identify them, get passionate about them.

I know that sometimes when you are fed up with life, passion can seem like a long distant dream, so don't get too discouraged if you don't yet know what you're passionate about. You get to have an exciting journey of discovery. Woohoo. (Come on, get enthusiastic.)

If you look for your passions, you'll find them; and deep down, I suspect you already have some inkling for what you're passionate about. Some passions come to you as you discover them; some are with you from childhood. Some lie buried in your heart, waiting for you to acknowledge them.

When I started exploring my passions I knew I was passionate about words (I loved to read and I wanted to write, even though I wouldn't - in fact I couldn't admit it), music (listening, singing, dancing to it, not playing it) and freedom (stories about women's freedoms being curtailed drove me wild. They still do).

I thought those things were too boring, too mundane, too tame to be my real passions. But I am still passionate about words and music and freedom - in fact, 2 of them are cornerstones of my business and the other one creates the soundtrack to my life.

When you're passionate about something, whatever it is, you bring life to that thing – your passion makes it come alive. Think back to your school days and remember a teacher who brought a subject alive – they were passionate about it. You've probably also experienced the opposite – a teacher who made quite an interesting subject snore-worthy (History of Economics lecturer, I'm talking to you).

Anyway, passions aren't necessarily fascinating all by themselves – it's your passion that animates it and makes it zing. I once watched 3 videos a Facebook friend posted about crochet. I have zero interest in crochet, but her passion and enthusiasm for the subject were so infectious, I got drawn in. We're back to owning your geeky side again – if your passions are nerdy, so what?

Discover those passions; make sure they play a part in your life. You can even arrange your life to revolve around your passions, which is so cool. Sometimes just making time for your passions does that for you without you realising. Honestly, it feels like I woke up one day and realised "Hey, I'm writing every day, and I help people create freedom in their lives, and I'm always listening to music and taking dance breaks".

It probably wasn't that much of a surprise really – I discovered my passions, made them a part of my life; and ultimately the foundations of my business. Whether that's an option for you right now or not, indulge your passions and just see where that takes you. You may just wake up one day and realise your life is all about what you're passionate about.

Enjoy your job

If you hate your job now, do your best to enjoy it anyway. Make it fun, look for things to enjoy, do what you can to make it better. Your job takes up 40 hours of your life every week (and if you're fed up and miserable, it's harder to job hunt), make that 40 hours as good as you can.

What's that you say? "There's no point because I'm leaving"? Yeah, I said that for 3 years too. Listen I don't give a hoot if you plan to leave next week - do what you can to make those 40 hours as enjoyable as possible. This is your life we're talking about here.

The irony is that we sometimes have this belief that we can't enjoy our job because if we do we won't want to leave, and we want to leave. That kind of thinking doesn't work. All that happens is that you get more and more brassed off with life, your confidence goes into your boots, and you can no more job-hunt than fly to the moon.

If you do your best to enjoy it as much as you can, you'll feel better, you'll have more energy, and you'll have more confidence to look for something better. AND in the meantime, while you're looking, you'll enjoy the job more. This is all relative too - if you enjoy your job 5/100 at the moment, making it 10/100 will be double the enjoyment.

Convinced? Want the how? Ok, try this: ask yourself "how much do I enjoy my job now on a scale of 1-100"; where 1 is 'I couldn't hate it more', and 100 is 'I love it I love it I love it I love it'. Don't overthink it, go with whatever number you intuitively come up with.

Once you've got your baseline number, ask yourself this "what can I do today/this week to bump this number up one or two points?" Ask that question every day/week and keep making little changes until you enjoy your job more. You might not get to love it (I never did), but it will be better than it was.

By the way, yes, you do know the answers you need. I know that - you are smarter than you give yourself credit for. Sometimes you just need to ask the right questions or give it more than 2 seconds thought to find those answers.

When I started to enjoy my job more (I probably got to about 60/100), I felt better, had more energy, was more confident, and within 3 months I'd left and got a new job. After 3 years of moaning about how much I hated my job. Sometimes it takes changing the energy and changing how you feel before you can change what you're doing.

Like I've said before, if it worked and felt good to just hate your job 40 hours a week, I'd say 'keep it up', but it doesn't – it sucks when you hate your job, so get lovin it up. Little bit by little bit figure out what would make it a little better, take action and improve your work life. It's easier to just keep being hacked off with it (I know, I did it for years, it's really easy), but it never makes it better.

It just makes you feel bad – hour after hour, day after day, year after year; and in some cases decade after decade. Don't let that be you. Do what you can to make it better. Even if your job sucks, even if your boss is a jackass, even if your colleagues are mean, even if your customers are idiots. Do what you can to make it better.

One of my clients had a job she hated with a passion, a boss she despised as a pointless, useless, spineless, stupid and vile person; colleagues who actively made her job harder; and customers who were nasty and did nothing but complain. She couldn't see how she could make it even a tiny bit better. So I asked her to just treat each person in front of her as if she liked them.

One at a time. That was it. She found that some of her customers were actually human; that her colleagues had thought she was the awkward, unfriendly one and once they understood what she needed from them, they were able to do it. Her boss was still a jackass. Maybe you can't have everything, eh? She went from 1/100 – really hating her job, to about 65/100 in a couple of months with a few small changes and she was astonished at how much difference it made to her life.

I wasn't. Work is a HUGE part of your life. It takes the majority of your waking hours. If you hate all those hours, that will seep into the rest of your life; and before you know it the only time you are not thinking about, talking about, moaning about and detesting work is when you're asleep. I know, I've been there. So stop the rot – find the ways to make a difference to your day and make it better than bloody awful. It's your life, it's your job, it's your choice.

Set new rules for your life

What rules have you set for yourself? What rules have you followed since you were 8 years old? No snoozing in the afternoon? No laughing or messing about in class (work)? Keep your nose to the grindstone? Don't wear zigzag tights with a flowery dress? (My friend's daughter just started dressing herself and it's amazing – she doesn't know the rules, so she breaks them with joy and flair.)

Do you colour in the lines? Do you walk with decorum? Do you sit like a laydee? Furthermore, does all this nonsense just stifle your spirit? Who the beep decided that blue and green should never be seen? And why for God's sake? (I like both green and blue, so I don't get it) Who says you can't write 2 paragraphs of questions? Ahem, maybe that person had a point.

Some rules make sense – don't run with scissors, tie your shoelaces before you start walking, be nice. Some make no sense – no snoozing in the day? No messing about or laughing in work time? Work so hard that you give yourself an ulcer? No, no and a thousand times, no. Maybe it's time to break a few rules?

What rules have you set yourself? You might have food rules, fashion rules, relationship rules, rules on fun (chores before playing, anyone?), work rules, things you're allowed to (and not allowed to) do at certain times. If those rules keep you safe and happy and within the law (getting arrested for breaking a rule is not joyous, it's daft), then keep them. If those rules constrict you, limit you, and make you glum, it's time to rewrite them.

Here are a few of my new rules:

"If you're tired, sleep, no matter what time of day it is."

"Afternoon energy dips require dance breaks."

"Yoga before I start work helps me concentrate."

"Having fun at work is essential - I'm working 40 hours a week, I'm damn well going to enjoy it"

"Drawing stick men is work too" (hooray for the illustrations in this book).

"If I enjoy it, do it. If I don't, don't do it."

"Doing the dance that goes with the song is mandatory."

"Easy-and-fun-work is the new hard-work."

"Instead of going from task to task without a break, have a mental palate cleanse in the form of dance, meditation, stretch or getting fresh air."

"It is perfectly acceptable to say no to invitations to things I don't want to do and suggest alternatives we'll both enjoy."

What new rules could you add? Remember, these are the rules for helping you love your life, not the rules to keep yourself under control.

Get rid of your debts

Debts eat your money and make you miserable. Get rid of them. Make a commitment right now to do it, and follow this easy formula: an easy to make monthly payment + extra payments when possible + low/no interest + NO ADDING TO THE DEBT = repayment.

Imagine for a second how good it would feel to not hand over half your money every month to your creditors, to be able to save it and spend it on YOU. Hazah! Yes, you might have to do without the big television and the designer jeans and the new shoes for a while, but trust me, it will be worth it.

Ok, I hear ya - you've got no spare money. I get it, I've been there. Let me underline part one of that formula for you: <u>an easy to make monthly payment</u> – a payment you can easily make. As long as it's enough to more than cover your minimum repayments (and if not, get some unbiased help from not for profit debt organisations in your country), it'll do for now.

It will still take time, there's no escaping that – it may even take years, but there is magic in starting to take action. When I decided to pay off my credit cards in 2006, the payment I could easily make was pitifully small and at that rate, it would have taken me 5 years to clear the debt. I started anyway, and the debt was gone in 2 years. It happens every time I commit to a financial goal. Magic happens when you commit.

A client of mine had a large debt he couldn't seem to get under control. When he looked at it in terms of the formula, he was trying to pay a big chunk every month which was more than he could easily afford, he never paid any extra, the debt had high interest and he was adding to the debt every month. Once he started following the formula, he could see the debt instantly begin to come down.

Although he felt the payment was not enough, it covered his minimum payment, and he paid extra whenever he could. He worked out it would take 10 years to pay it off at that rate, but magic started to happen, and the debt was halved in 18 months. The same has happened with every client I've shared this formula with.

Once you make the decision to get shot of your debts, all sorts of things will swing into action to help you. If the miracles don't seem to appear instantly, don't worry – keep making your easy payment on a low-interest plan and making extra payments when you can and not putting anything else on the cards; and you will clear that debt in time.

We've become a society of people who want it all *now*. Including having our debts paid off, but although you can rack up fabulous amounts of debt in an afternoon of shopping, paying for it will take time. It's worth taking that time, it's worth making that commitment.

It feels truly lovely to be able to keep the money you earn, and it's hard to fall in love with life when you're working for your credit card company to pay off things you wore to a party 8 years ago and can't even remember now. Trust me, I know.

Clutter clear

Clutter makes life harder - you can't find anything, you're surrounded by mess, and every time you open a cupboard, a hundred things fall out. Bah. Even if it's not quite that bad, clutter creates stuck energy (yeah, I know it's a bit woo-woo, so what? It's still true). You can feel the energy change when you do a spring clean - it's clearer, cleaner, lighter.

So clear your clutter. Whether you wait until it gets too much and then go crazy throwing away all your stuff into 20 black bags when you have PMT (as I used to), or you keep a more consistent eye on your clutter and clear out daily, weekly or monthly, clearing your clutter will make you happier.

If you don't love it or use it, chuck it.

By the way, don't make this a big painful chore – make it fun, make it easy. I like to clutter clear in 10-minute bursts, with music playing in the background – it's a lot easier than doing it for a whole weekend, and I can do another 10 minutes tomorrow. I'll just pick a particular hotspot, like my desk or the bedside table – they seem to magnetise clutter - and I clear just that area for now.

Clearing clutter is not about being a neat freak and living in a show home (not possible if you actually *live* in your house, especially if other people live with you). It's also not about getting down to 100 possessions (even when backpacking around Australia I never managed that – I always had stuff tied to the outside of my rucksack).

It's about letting go of the stuff that is messing up your head and your house. It has the surprising effect of getting you unstuck – whenever I get stuck in my work, I look around and see the mayhem I'm surrounded by. After 10 minutes clearing said mayhem, I get unstuck; or at least I can find whatever I'm working on, which helps.

Don't forget your cyber clutter too – unsubscribe from e-mails you don't read, delete anything older than a month (when I get e-mail overwhelm, I sometimes just delete the lot), unfollow Twitter accounts you aren't interested in, unfriend people you don't actually know on Facebook.

My current cyber clutter clearing project is unfollowing on twitter – I'm trying to clean up my tweet-stream so I can actually see people I like and am interested in. So, every time I log in, I pick someone to unfollow. Soon I hope to be able to go to twitter and be interested in all the people I'm following. Like physical clutter, cyber clutter is irritating, makes it difficult to find things you actually want, and can drive a person barking mad.

Whether it's virtual clutter or clutter that falls on your head whenever you open cupboard doors, let go of the things you don't need – give them away, sell them, delete them. Make space in your life for the things you do want and make space to love your life without having to wade through tons of mess first.

Either give up your bad habits or enjoy them

Life's too short to beat yourself up. When you're ready to stop your bad habits, you'll stop. When people hear I'm a coach, one of the things they often ask is if I can help them give up something.

(Honestly, I'm grateful that they've heard of coaching but the link between coaching and bad habits needs to be broken, people. Coaching is about bringing the best from yourself, always. It's not about making yourself conform to a world of shoulds. Interestingly, when you start getting the best from yourself, the bad habits fall away, because you're busy feeling good and bad habits feel bad.)

Anyway, back to helping people give something up. My reply is always "Do you want to?" If they don't, I say no, I can't help. I wouldn't even try. The answer is almost always 'no, I don't want to' – I know that before I ask the question because if they really wanted to give up their bad habit, they would.

I smoked for about 15 years, and I tried to give up for 10 of them. I failed, continuously, for 8 years or so. I didn't want to give up enough to actually do it. Then I gave up giving up smoking which I was much more successful at. Then there came a day where I wanted to give up more than I wanted to smoke. I've probably had 5 cigarettes since that day.

It was so easy, I couldn't believe it. But that's the thing: if you don't really want to give up smoking or drinking or dancing on tables or eating cake, you probably won't. So instead of beating yourself up and making yourself feel like a total failure and waste of good air, enjoy your bad habits.

And no, I don't mean give yourself lung cancer or pickle your liver in vodka. You can enjoy bad habits in moderation you know. If your life is at stake, it is a powerful motivator to WANT to stop. My mom had a heart attack in her 50's, and her doctor said: "You don't smoke anymore". She had never wanted to give up, but once it was a choice between heart health and smoking, it was a no brainer. She gave up instantly.

Sometimes our bad habits are not entirely our own – we smoke and drink and eat more because the people around us are. So check your bad habits are really your own, that you're not just doing them to fit in or because you need a crutch (there are better ways to get confident and love life than alcohol – and I say that as someone who used alcohol as a confidence boost for years) or because someone is beer-bullying you. Get clear about whether *you* want your bad habit. If you do, enjoy it.

Once I'd decided not to give up smoking, I did decide to cut down, because there was a lot about the habit I didn't like (the smell, the cost, the fact it was making my throat bad), which ultimately made it easier to give up entirely. Maybe your bad habits could be released the same way? Without the guilt and self-recrimination, and with ease and enjoyment, gentleness and calmness?

Learn to say NO

No is not a word to be scared of hearing, or of saying. The trouble is, most of us attach a whole made up story to the word no. If someone says no to us, they don't love us. If we say no to someone, we're letting them down. No = rejection.

Only it doesn't, not really. It just means no. "No thank you", if you want to put it more politely. Your waiter offers you coffee at the end of your meal, 'no'. It's not a rejection of the coffee or of the waiter, he's not going to go into the kitchen and weep, it's just 'no thank you'. No story, no drama, just 'no'.

No is actually quite easy to say. Want me to hit you on the head with a cricket bat? 'Hell, no'. Do you like Marmite? 'Hell, NO'. Do you want to be miserable all your life? 'Hell, no'. See? Easy.

You don't have to respond to every request with "Hell NO!" You can say:

"No, thank you"

"Let me check my diary" (then check it and say "sorry, I can't")

"Okay, you want me to do X, then let's have a look at what I will need to drop to be able to fit it in" (for bosses)

"I don't fancy that, but I'd love to do X with you instead" (for friends/lovers asking you to do something with them)

Or you could just try a smile, and a "No."

In an episode of the Big Bang Theory, the guys take it in turns to ask Sheldon's very beautiful sister out. With a sunny smile, she gently says 'no'. In this case, it is a rejection, but it's done so sweetly. No explanations, no nastiness, no 'Hell NO', just a smile and a 'no'.

What's the story you make up about the word no? Is it rude? Will it lose you friends, opportunities, jobs? Is it a nasty thing to say? Does it mean the world will hate you? None of these are true by the way. No is just no. No, I don't want coffee. No, I cannot do those extra hours. No, I don't want to go to the extremely boring event. No, I can't chair the time-consuming committee.

No means that you have time and space for rest, relaxation and things that make your heart sing. It means you're not filling up your days with stuff you wish you said 'no' to. It means you are able to say 'yes' more. I have had so many clients whose lives are so full to the brim that they don't have room for their friends and family.

Once they learn to say 'no' to some of the things that are taking up time and space, they find they are able to take time with the people they care about. Plus, they do not feel they are running around with their hair on fire. If you love to be busy and always on the run, good for you, but if you notice that being constantly busy is making you ill and stressed, maybe it's time for a bit of constructive 'no'ing?

Since I started having energy problems (CFS/MS related), I have used this strategy for everything I am asked: "Let me check my diary and get back to you". I don't just check the date of the event or appointment, I check the days before and after. I cannot do more than one thing a day, or I'll be exhausted. After certain things, I need recovery time – either later that day or the next day.

So I check all of this before booking anything in. If I don't, I'll end up wiped out and not wanting or able to do anything for weeks. Although I have always blamed this on my energy issues, I have found that 90% of my clients also need this down time after being busy doing. Which of course, they never gave themselves, because it is normal to be too busy and stressed out. (Only it's not, of course it's not, it's crazy.)

Once these clients started to be more attentive to what they needed in terms of downtime, they started saying no. Every one of them then reported that they enjoyed the other things they were doing because they had the energy and brain space to do so. Every one of them found the time, because of no, to do things they couldn't fit in before learning to say no.

No isn't rude, or mean, it doesn't make you a terrible, selfish person. It is just no. No allows yes to other things. So it's worth learning to say no.

Quit judging your life

So, you're sat with a rug around your legs like a little old dear working on bank holiday Monday? So, you're not in charge of the universe? So, your love life resembles either a soap opera or the tale of a nun? So, you're not doing the work you love to do? So, you hate your job and you have for years? So, you're not perfect? So, your life sucks?

Stop judging it. Stop comparing it to your friends and acquaintances, and worse, to random celebs you don't know. Stop looking at Facebook and thinking everyone else's life is so much more exciting and interesting than yours. First of all, most people put their best face out to the world (except the ones who like to share every detail of how awful their life is, and that's often exaggerated too).

Secondly, you can't know what's really going on in someone else's head. I've had friends go bankrupt, get hospitalised, get divorced, have breakdowns; and I thought their life was peachy. We have some crazy notion that everything has to be perfect in our lives; that we have to have achieved all our dreams by the time we're 26; that our life has to be glamorous and fabulous and full of interesting events and enviable parties.

Or whatever your version of that is. If this behaviour helped – massively judging our lives and comparing ourselves to others, I'd say 'go to it', but it doesn't. It's depressing. It makes us feel bad about ourselves and our lives and doesn't usually get us to make any changes, because when we judge something, it's like a pronouncement of "this is how it is. The end".

Also, it is often an exaggeration. It's a bank holiday Monday here in the UK as I write this, and I am sitting, with a blanket over my knees like a little old dear, writing instead of being out doing something more interesting. I have my reasons, but when I just judge that (as I did earlier today), I feel bad that my life isn't interesting (after one bank holiday spent writing?), that I'm like a little old lady (who says that's a terrible thing anyway?), that I'm such a saddo and have no life. Really?

Ok, some people may consider me a saddo and boring (but that's their opinion and they're welcome to it), but I chose to spend the day doing this, and now I'm judging myself (and my life) for it. Unfairly judging it at that. Harshly even. And it didn't help me in any way at all. It put me into a funk for a while.

Then I realised if I really wanted to be doing anything else, I could. It's not like someone nailed my feet to the floor in my house. So I got over it. The more you make sweeping judgements about your life (harsh and unfair judgements), the less likely you are to change it, and the more time you will spend picking yourself up out of a funk.

So what if you're sitting like a granny with a blanket around your legs? So what if you'd rather spend the day reading than partying? So what if you're not in charge of the universe? So what if your life isn't as interesting as it was when you were 18? (Thank God mine isn't, I can't handle the hangovers and lack of sleep now.)

Quit judging your life (and yourself). If there's something you genuinely don't like about your life, change it. Otherwise, you might as well enjoy sitting writing on a Bank holiday with your blanket around your knees like a little old dear.

Part 6:

Feeling Good

Lighten up

Short of death or serious illness, there's no reason to lose your sense of humour. Taking yourself and your life too seriously is a great way to *not* love your life. Lighten Up. Take it easy, see the funny side, the bright side, the comedy in life. Don't make everything so significant.

Most of us are really hard on ourselves, set ourselves impossible expectations and rigid rules (designed to keep our noses firmly to the grindstone, not conducive to falling in love with life). When we do this, we make life so much harder.

If this helped to be super tough on yourself and take everything very seriously, I'd say "Go ahead, that's really working for you". Of course, it doesn't help. Life is a dance of joyful discovery. Every time you get all serious and start making everything so significant and tense, it feels like walking uphill through treacle with steel boots on.

The moment you lighten up, life gets easier again. So what exactly does to 'lighten up' mean? My definition is "To chill out, relax, stop worrying, enjoy life, be cheerful and silly, and take life lightly". Auntie Google adds: "To make light or lighter; illuminate or brighten"; "To be luminous; shine"; "To take matters less seriously"; "To make more cheerful". Lovely.

It's not always easy of course when the days are dark, the weight of the world is on your shoulders and you are stressed and on the serious treadmill of life. But every time you remember to Lighten Up, you are strengthening your Lighten Up muscles and making it easier to choose to be light again, and again, and again.

It's worth remembering too, that most things are either a good experience or a good story. When I was in Australia, the things I loved were the sunsets, the lovely people I met, the beaches, the fun times. The things my friends enjoyed most were the bad things – the terrifying skyfall, the disastrous bike ride - they were horrible experiences, but they made great stories – especially when I lightened up and saw the funny side (after the bruises healed).

Lightening up can also help you to be more effective and efficient in your life. When you're tense and stressed and agitated and wired, your brain doesn't work as well. When you're being super hard on yourself, it makes it difficult for you to access your creative genius and your connection to inspiration.

I had a client who was trying to set up a business doing something she really loved, but she was taking it so seriously, she'd squashed all her joy, creativity and enthusiasm. I asked her to lighten up and just have some fun with it. After 6 months of struggling, within a month of lightening up, she'd got her first clients and was up and running.

Not only that, she was enjoying her life again. Sometimes life does throw circumstances and events at you that seem to call for serious. But most things really aren't worth losing your sense of humour for – they're momentary, you'll have forgotten about them in a few weeks/months/years anyway. So lighten up, don't let everything become so significant, have a laugh about the ridiculous things that happen in life and take life lightly.

Don't wait to get happy

Don't ever wait 'til X happens to be happy. Be happy first, otherwise you're wasting good happy time for no good reason. It's such a common idea: I'll be happy when I have a good job; I'll be happy when I've paid off my debts; when I've got my dream house; when I've lost weight; when I've met Mr Right; when Mr Right picks up his socks; when the moon is in Sagittarius.

Why wait? Why wait for life to be perfect? Why wait for all your ducks to line up in a neat and tidy row? Why wait for the impossible? Hey, I'm not saying you won't get a good job, pay off your debts, lose weight, meet Mr Right and have him pick up socks in your dream house under a Sagittarian moon – you will. If that's what you want. Then you'll find another excuse to postpone happiness.

You'll want to get a better job, be financially secure, get fit again after the Christmas blow-out, get a bigger house/car/dishwasher. It is our nature to desire more. We want, and then we get and we want something else. I have a list of desires - from trips I want to take to new underwear. These desires never diminish, I always want something.

So if I wait until I have everything I ever wanted to be happy, first of all, I'll be waiting for a LONG time, and secondly I'm wasting happy time. You can be happy and broke. You can be happy and single. You can be happy and in a job you know you'll leave. You can be happy and in your pre-dream house. You can be happy at any weight.

Happiness is not dependant on outside circumstances. It's dependant on you. I had a client once who, in her own words, "had everything I ever wanted" – the house, the job, the kids, the husband, the car, the effing big television, the top-of-the-range appliances, the respect of colleagues, a circle of successful friends. And she was utterly miserable.

She was waiting for her shopping list of desires to be complete, and then she would be happy. Only she wasn't. When she stopped hiding behind 'I'll be happy when…' and decided to be happy today, she enjoyed her life more (and by extension, so did everyone around her – if you're miserable, it affects your kids, your husband, your friends, your colleagues).

It really is that simple – just stop waiting until X happens to be happy. Be happy today. Without the perfect body or husband or house or job or hair. Sometimes we think it's better to stay unhappy because that will encourage us to get out of the relationship or job or life we don't love. It really doesn't work that way.

Instead what happens is that our confidence starts to erode, woe and worry become habitual, and we are LESS likely to get out. The better you feel, the easier it is to move on. Plus, why wait to be happy? Ok, so your job sucks. It happens. We all have that at some point in life. Don't postpone your joy because of it.

Be happy on the way to your desired life. Be happy on the journey. I know, it's not always easy to do, but it starts with a decision to stop putting off your happiness, and make today a happy day. Even if your ducks aren't sitting in a row and your life isn't perfect, be happy anyway.

I also think this includes the idea of saving your best stuff for when the Queen comes to visit. I get why this was a thing last century – we didn't have the throwaway culture we have today, stuff was more expensive and less easy to get. (Young people – did you know that shops used to shut on Saturday afternoon and not open again until Monday?)

Now, it's a false economy – we leave things so long that they never get used. So wear your best perfume, use the silk sheets, put on your party dress on a Tuesday, use the good toiletries and the soft loo roll. Don't save it all for best. Don't wait, your life is happening now – get enjoying it.

Wake up with a smile

Let me be clear - I am NOT a morning person - I am not naturally chipper and chirpy before I've been awake for an hour or so, but I do know that *how you're woken up* makes a big difference to how you feel. One of my biggest rants in life is about the utter moron who thought waking up to an incessant "beep. Beep. Beep." was a good idea. Honestly, who wants to wake up like that?

For years, I would be jarred out of sleep by this awful, offensive noise, already in a foul mood because A: I'd been woken up, and B: I'd been woken up in such a rude and objectionable way. Bah. Cue the morning grumps.

As I say, I'm no morning person at the best of times BUT wake me up with something that doesn't set my teeth on edge and annoy me before I'm even fully awake and I'm a much nicer person to be around. My preference is to wake up naturally - when I've had enough sleep, or my bladder needs emptying, I'll wake up all by myself.

Sometimes that's not practical as I have to be up at the crack of a sparrow's fart. On those days, I have a CD alarm (the greatest invention of the last 300 years) with music I like. Not some annoying DJ who's far too cheerful at asleep o'clock in the morning (there's nothing worse to a non-morning person than a chirpy morning person).

Aside: Dear morning people, rein in your chirpiness in the morning around us non-morning people - you may not understand us, but that will not stop us hitting you with a chair. Ahem, anyway, where was I?

Ah yes, music I like. Here's how I make up my CD (or playlist nowadays):

The first song is a nice, mellow, lovely song to gently coax me out of sleep, and soothing enough that I can get an extra 3-4 minutes kip if necessary. From there, the music gets progressively more upbeat, until we get to the likes of Beyoncé, the Spice Girls (hey, we've established before, I am not cool) and the Black Eyed Peas (who can stay in bed when Crazy in Love/Spice up Your Life/Pump It comes on the stereo?).

Alakazam, I'm up, and I'm relatively cheerful. I'm still a grouch - like I say, I'm not a morning person, but I am not livid at having been disagreeably awakened.

As you can see, I'm pretty passionate about this - what I'm saying is **wake up in the best way for you** – in a way that allows you to wake up feeling good, not in a way that makes you start the day with a racing heart and smashing your alarm clock to pieces on your mind.

Find your movement happy place

What is your favourite way to move your body? What's your movement happy place? I'm not talking about going to the gym for 80 hours a week, or running 10 miles a day (unless that's what you enjoy, in which case, go for it). Movement (some people call it exercise) does make you feel better. When you move, you feel good, you wake up the endorphins (feel-good hormones) in your body.

We've got the equivalent of a happy pill right there inside us, use it.

For some of us, the very thought of exercise brings us out in hives. Forget that – don't think of it as exercise, just move your body in a way that feels good to you. Dance, skip, walk in nature, swim, chase the dog / kids / husband around the garden, do star jumps while waiting for your pasta to cook, climb a tree, play a sport (to play, not to exercise), do cartwheels, do yoga, whatever appeals to you to invite those endorphins out to play.

Often people object to exercise because it reminds them of god-awful sports classes at school. I can totally relate – I was terrible at sport at school. Couldn't run or throw or score or play a decent backhand, but that doesn't mean I can't enjoy moving my body now. We're not talking 'no pain, no gain' here, or 'feel the burn' (oh hell no) – I believe in 'no pain, no pain' and 'feel the joy'.

I also hear a lot "I have tried *everything* and I hate all body movement". Hmm. There may be someone out there who genuinely has tried every single thing possible and hates it all, but most people have tried 4/5 max, and they're all a similar genre – usually cardio. Hey, when I go on the cross-trainer, I'm not normally high on endorphins – I'm hot, sweaty and have really wobbly legs. (I still enjoy it though – it's inexplicable.)

In the spirit of full disclosure here, I will tell you this – I sometimes have to force my sorry behind out the door to walk the dog, or to do yoga, or to dance, but when I do I ALWAYS feel better. I feel calmer, I feel happier, my body feels good, my mind feels good, I'm more connected to my heart and soul. So even if I'd rather be sat eating chocolates on a chaise longue all day (and if I had a chaise longue, I would), I make myself move my butt anyway.

Note: there is a difference between overcoming a little resistance and pushing yourself to move when what you really need is rest – learn the difference, your health will thank you for it.

You need to find your move your body happy place – try something you've always fancied – belly dance, yoga class, running club, tennis, badminton, trampolining (friends with kids are good for this one), 5 aside football, martial arts, basketball, netball, Zumba, read a book while on a static bike, or just put on music you like and have a bop around your kitchen. It's fun, it's good for you, it has all the health benefits doctors waffle on about (but that's no reason not to do it).

Loving your life is hard if you feel sluggish and have no energy, and moving your body will help you feel more energised, it'll help clear your mind, it will wake up tired muscles, it will help your body feel good. And if you pick the right things, you will have fun too.

Champagne moments

Do you ever listen to cricket (the sport, not the insect)? If you do, you may know that one of the things the Test Match Special commentary team do is to nominate 'champagne moments' of the match – special moments which warrant a cork pop and a raised glass. I love this idea, and I think we should all do this all day every day – nominate champagne moments throughout the day.

Joy lives in small moments that we often miss in the hustle and bustle of our lives. Our achievements also get lost in the day to day of living. We tend to only notice the *big* joys and the *big* achievements, and as they only come along a few times a year max, we rarely feel we have anything to celebrate.

That's such a shame, because most days there is something to celebrate – a project that has progress made on it, a pound lost, a phone call to a friend, a canny purchase of fabulous shoes, a hug with your partner or kids, sunshine, the dog obeying a command, the partner or kids doing the washing up.

All the small things that make up a life of small joys. So instead of missing them all, and feeling like there is very little in life to celebrate, why not start a practice of nominating champagne moments every day? You don't have to drink champers every day (or at all – I don't), the practice is to celebrate, not become a total lush. You could raise your evening cup of tea to the champagne moment of the day.

Every day, notice all the small things you enjoy, all the small things you achieve, all the moments of happiness and joy that would normally pass you by and designate each one a champagne moment. These champagne moments can be anything – stopped yourself punching your boss in the face? Champagne moment darling. Get a good parking space? Champagne moment. Found the perfect outfit for a night out? Champagne moment.

Then you can choose your favourite moment of the day and designate it today's champagne moment. One of my clients kept a diary of her daily champagne moments, and it makes her laugh to look back through and see what lovely things have happened every day (most of which she's forgotten a few short weeks later).

My champagne moment nominations so far today are: sitting in the sunshine doing my morning pages, a great session with a client this morning, a bird flying into the window and being ok, attaching ribbon to the window so birds won't fly into it anymore (love it when I achieve something practical), recording a great meditation for myself, adding 3 new chapters to this book.

What are your champagne moment nominations for today? And every day.

Wake up and smell the waste of time

Back in the days before 24-hour life, people had time to do stuff. To talk, to read, to have a bath, to putter about the house, to cook, to do all sorts of things. Of course, they couldn't watch TV on 524 channels or check up on friends they've never met online, or watch videos of crazy cats, so they had time.

Although there is talk of the world speeding up and us needing to add another second, or day, or something to our year to make the seasons go right, we're not going to gain enough time to make a real difference to our days. One day in 1000 years, or whatever it is, isn't going to give you the time to do your favourite things or start a business or write a book.

Maybe reclaiming the wasted time in your day will? It's easy to waste hours and weeks and your life in front of the TV or computer, but does it make you feel good? Pay attention to how you feel. I love surfing the net and watching TV, but there comes a point where I'm no longer loving it, and I'm just compulsively carrying on.

At some point, I wake up and realise I've just wasted an entire day watching 12 episodes of a series from the '80s; or surfing the net and can't remember one thing I looked at. Get into the habit of checking in with yourself every half hour or so: is this activity feeling good? Am I still enjoying it? Is there something else I'd rather do with my time?

If you often find yourself bored and checking Facebook, Twitter, or endlessly channel surfing, this will be a revelation for you – maybe that time could be better spent doing something you actually find fun? Maybe the time you spend doing things you're not bothered about could be used to read a book, to learn to paint, to spend more time with friends and family, to dance?

If you love crazy cat videos and spending hours on Facebook or Twitter or Pinterest or parked in front of the TV, then continue. I'm not the internet or TV police. Nevertheless if you, like me, have a tendency to lose hours of your life moodling fruitlessly, you might want to look at some of the things you never have time for and do them instead.

Stop and smell the bread

I know, the usual saying is about flowers and roses, but is there any better smell than fresh bread? I was on holiday in Ibiza many moons ago, and when coming home from the clubs every morning at 5 am, the bakery was just opening and that fresh bread smell was heaven. 20-eek years ago, and I still smile when I think about that memory.

Anyway, this tip is not about putting your nose into the nearest loaf of course (unless you want to), but about pausing occasionally to notice your life. Notice the moments of joy as you dash from place to place. I get it, you're terribly busy and important, but a pause in your day won't cause the world to fall down.

Get into the habit of just pausing for a moment when something good is happening. Feel the sun on your face. Enjoy how a hug with a loved one feels. Give the person you're with your full attention. When your favourite song comes on the radio, stop what you're doing and sing and dance along. Wear your best clothes, use your best tableware. Smell the bread.

Be here, in this moment, in your life. You're reading this book – are you enjoying it? (If not, please put it down, life's too damn short.) Are you comfortable? Take a deep breath and just notice what's happening around you. Are you half here now and half running through your to-do list? Are you worrying about yesterday and planning tomorrow, or are you here, now, in this moment?

It can feel difficult when we're so used to dashing about like road-runner on speed to slow down and take a moment, but that moment only has to last one breath. Whenever you remember to, stop and take one breath. Hear the birds sing, watch the world go by, smell that really nice aftershave. Just for one breath.

Dance with this moment. This moment right now. Whenever you notice you're frowning or fed up or bored, notice what's good about this moment. Fall in love with this moment, right now. Do this often enough and you will be in love with your life.

Who do you think you're talking to?

Does any of this sound familiar:
"You suck"
"Oh my God, you're such an idiot"
"You look terrible"
"Well, that was a massive failure, you useless cretin"
"For Pete's sake, are you always going to be so useless?"
"Again? We're in this situation again? When will you ever learn?"
"Your belly/bottom/legs/boobs/arms/feet are disgusting"
"See, I told you not to eat that cake fatty"
These are all (sanitised) examples of things my clients have told me they say to themselves on a daily basis. Let's imagine for a moment that instead of happening in your own head, these undermining comments were coming from your beloved. How long would this go on before you A: Told them to get stuffed B: Punched them or C: Left them.

Hopefully, it wasn't an awfully long time. Telling yourself to get stuffed isn't that effective, nor is punching yourself and leaving yourself is impossible without mind-altering drugs or mental health issues. So you're stuck with you, and your spiteful comments to yourself.

Or are you?

Do you know what? Most of us really want the best for ourselves deep down, and the catty comments are our way of motivating ourselves. I don't know about you, but I don't find nastiness that motivating. It makes me feel bad about myself, and I am less likely to do whatever I'm trying to motivate myself to do. Once we realise this though we can change what we're doing.

I am motivated by encouragement and by building me up, not knocking me down. I shared this with a client who said they couldn't imagine not being so mean to themselves. I asked if they would talk to their best friend in the world that way. Of course, she wouldn't, unless she wanted to not be her best friend anymore.

So I asked her to pretend she was talking to her best friend. Instead of telling herself she was fat, lazy, would never make it, and had really bad hair, she started to say "You are gorgeous, I believe in you 100% and I know you can do this. Plus, you really need to call the hairdresser." (Sometimes there's truth in the bitchiness, but you can put it lovingly, right?)

She was amazed at the difference it made. Instead of feeling alone and unsupported (as well as fat, lazy and like she'd never make it), she started to feel supported, encouraged, confident and have faith that she could and would do what she wanted (and have great hair).

When you think about it, it's not rocket-science – most of us know that getting the best out of someone involves positivity, support, reassurance and reward (think of the bosses you worked really well for and liked - they were probably this kind of boss), and yet we don't apply it to ourselves. Well, I'm here to give you permission to get the best from yourself by building yourself up, not knocking yourself down.

By the way, beating yourself up for beating yourself up is kind of missing the point, so give yourself a break. Most people are hard on themselves. Now you know there's another way, you can try that until it becomes a habit, and that will take as long as it takes. If you've got 40+ years of programming to undo, it's not going to be instantaneous.

Appreciate

Be grateful. Count your blessings. Notice how lucky you are. Yeah, I know some of us have a knee-jerk reaction to gratitude - we know we should be grateful, our parents told us we didn't know we were born, blah, blah, blah. But our life is pretty sucky. Right? Wrong.

The very fact that you are reading this tells me that you have a computer/phone/tablet (or all 3), and therefore access to wisdom from across the world (and stupid computer games that steal *hours* of your life); that you probably have running water, running WARM water at that; that you probably have a roof over your head and clothes on your back; that you can go to a supermarket and choose from 86 types of cereal; and that you probably have so much stuff that you have nowhere to put it all.

We take our lives so much for granted that it is shocking (when you think about it) - I have been known to complain that I can't afford new Adidas trainers. There are people out there who have no shoes. I have been known to complain that I have no money to go out for dinner. There are 25000 people dying every day for want of any food at all.

I know, I get it, it's all relative, and I'm not here to make you feel bad. That would completely ruin the point of this book after all. So you may not feel that you are so fortunate right now for any of those things I mentioned. So try feeling appreciation for what you DO appreciate.

It could be that you're grateful for the snack machine at work. Or grateful for your favourite TV program.

Or grateful that the working day ends eventually. Or grateful that you have music in the car on your commute home. Or grateful for a good bra. I'm not asking you to shout 'Hallelujah' and fall on your knees. I'm asking you to notice your blessings, whatever they are. Big or small, it doesn't matter – it just matters that it's true for you in this moment.

Today, I was in the shower feeling a bit meh, a bit down and fed up and not loving life. So I decided to list a few things I felt grateful for. Just in the shower alone, I came up with 20 things (hot running water, an abundance of shampoo, the use of all my limbs, stout walls so I don't freeze my backside off in the shower, toothpaste that doesn't make me gag (it's a problem I have), soft, warm towels to dry myself, and so on).

Within 2 minutes, I felt better. I realised how lucky I am. Even before I started on the rest of my house, I was filled with a beautiful feeling of gratitude and luckiness and joy. It's one of my favourite exercises, to look around me and list what I'm grateful for that I can see. My desk alone yields 30-odd things every time. (That's partly because it's pretty cluttered, but that's another story.)

Try it. Look around you now and look for things you're grateful for – are the windows and walls keeping out the rain? Do you have a pet close by keeping an eye on you and reminding you to stop work and get outside to play now and again? Do you have plentiful clean water? A comfortable chair under your bum? Adequate clothing/heating/air con for the temperature where you are? An abundance of books/music/DVD's/stationery/tech stuff?

Sometimes it's only when we face adversity (or even just mild discomfort) that we realise how lucky we are and appreciate the things we take for granted. Like when you've had a stinking cold and you can breathe through your nose and sleep again. Aaah, the appreciation of the simple breath.

Life may not be perfect, but learning to appreciate what you DO have feels good, and the better you feel, the better life gets.

Learn to choose how you feel

Did you know that you can choose how to feel most of the time? You can make choices about how you react, about how you respond, and ultimately about how you feel. You can choose to have the hump with your boss because they're being an asshat, or you can choose to let it go and feel good anyway.

You can choose to sit in a traffic jam muttering and scowling and grumbling, or you can choose to sing and dance and have a little car party on your own. I was stuck on the motorway a few years ago in very slow moving traffic, and I looked around to see lots and lots of fed up faces.

People were scowling, muttering angrily into their phones. One memorable guy looked livid and was driving as close as possible to the guy in front, which was utterly pointless as the guy in front had nowhere to go, there were a thousand or so other cars in his way.

No one looked happy at all. I was a bit irritated by it, yes, but I wasn't livid, and it's not worth getting your blood pressure up for. So I decided to have a car party. I turned up the radio and started singing and dancing in my car (just top half dancing, my feet were still driving). I grinned happily at everyone I passed, and I enjoyed the 2 hours I was stuck in slow moving traffic.

I could have focused on the fact that I was hungry, I would be late getting home, that I hate being stuck in traffic, but I chose to chill out and be a happy face in a sea of miserable faces. I like to think I brought a little joy to that corner of the motorway (well, they were laughing at me anyway).

This is not about avoiding how you feel – if you are angry or hurt or sad, you're allowed to feel those things, and in fact it's essential that you do feel how you feel, and let that emotion move through you instead of getting stuck inside and leading to a volcanic expression of temper, nervous breakdown, or illness. Ignoring your feelings isn't a good way to fall in love with life.

I'm talking about the propensity to fall into low-level irritation and mild fed-up-ness when you have a choice to respond differently. Having said that, this is possible even in the harshest of circumstances, as evidenced by Victor Frankl, incarcerated in concentration camps because of his race.

"I understood how a man who has nothing left in this world still may know bliss, be it only for a brief moment"

Most of us, thank God, are never put in such extreme circumstances, so making a choice on how to feel is much easier, comparatively. It sometimes doesn't feel that way, but remember Victor Frankl and remind yourself if he can do it, so can you.

One of my clients was in a situation where she went to work every day to be confronted with a boss "with a face like a spanked arse", and even if she was in a good mood when she went in to work, as soon as she saw the miserable face of her boss, she could feel good cheer leaving her, like air from a popped balloon.

I suggested she choose to be MORE cheerful in response. (I would not have suggested this if the boss had been ill or grieving, but she had just got in a glum, grumpy rut.) Being more cheerful in response to someone else's gloom has the effect of intensifying your own cheerfulness, lightening the energy, and sometimes even cheering the other person up. That's not the point of the exercise though – the point is to choose how you feel and act that way, not be brought down by someone else.

I know, it's easier said than done, but it's fun, it's a game, and sometimes has surprising consequences. Another client did this with a colleague who was known for being downcast and dejected and was avoided by most of the office. It took a while to warm this colleague up, but my client discovered under the grim façade a woman of wit and warmth.

Just as doom and gloom can be contagious, so can joy and good cheer. So choose the good cheer.

Be inspired by the positive stuff happening in the world

One of the things I am most exasperated by in life is the news. It's always so flipping negative. The news media delights in pulling people down, in reporting facts in the worst possible light and in telling us all horror stories about the way the world works. No wonder a lot of people think the world is a bad place full of bad people doing corrupt, dishonest and evil things.

But what they don't report on is the GOOD news. Not just 'the economy is up ½ a percent', but stories of courage, of innovation, of deep love and inspiration. Watching the mainstream news, one would assume that 90% of the population are liars, thieves, despots, cheats and evil dictators. They're not (pause a moment while I stand upon my soapbox).

The vast majority of people are good. Just look at the people you know – are they unscrupulous frauds and sociopathic murderers? I am guessing (and really rather hoping) not. I am guessing that they are nice people doing their best in the world. People who are kind and generous and who will get the elderly neighbours' newspaper every day or take a friend to the hospital for their x-ray.

Normal people. Watching the mainstream news, you'd be hard-pressed to find a normal person. Ok, I get that getting newspapers and taking friends to x-rays isn't really news. Still, there are people out there doing interesting and newsworthy positive stuff. When I rule the world, the mainstream news will of course report on nutters who are trying to start wars and cheating, lying politicians, but then they'll move onto the really interesting things.

The projects that are saving lives. The people who are innovating and coming up with new and exciting ideas to make the world a better place. Scientists and environmentalists and innovators and philanthropists who are doing cool stuff that deserves to be reported. If this type of thing interests you, check out www.ted.com – they have talks from interesting, influential people doing good stuff in the world – in their words, ideas worth spreading. Inspiring stuff.

Stuff that when you watch it makes you hopeful and excited and positive instead of despairing for the future of our world. THAT'S what the news should be about <Steps down off soapbox.>

If you spend your days consuming news, you will have a skewed view of this world. As I do. I spend my days consuming inspiration so I believe in the goodness of humanity. I believe for every corrupt, lying, warmongering nutter, there are thousands of loving, clever, kind, wonderful people – some of whom are doing incredible, inspirational work in the world.

I would much rather have my perspective skewed in a positive, hopeful direction, rather than believe that the world is heading to hell in a handbasket. For a start, it means I am not fearful of the world ending (unless I'm in a plane then, irrationally, I am). Also, it means that these inspiring, wonderful people make me believe in possibility, in innovation, in wonder, in a good future.

I'm inspired to do interesting things with my life because I see that being modelled for me by thousands of people doing awesome things. Open your eyes and see that this world is full of possibility and talent and opportunity and love and genius. Find people and organisations who inspire you. Find stories that move you and encourage you to do some good in the world, instead of the ones that have you shrugging your shoulders and saying 'what's the point?'

Because those people who inspire you, they're just like you. If they can do amazing things with their lives, so can you. Let their achievements encourage you to reach for more in your life and get inspired.

Participate in life

I have a confession to make: this is a tip that I wrote for me. I have a tendency to get a bit caught up in working and normal life stuff and forget to get out of the house. It doesn't help that I am, by nature, a hermit, and especially in winter, I would much rather stay in than go out.

Yet if I do the hermitess thing for too long, I start to go a bit stir crazy and get stressed out and have meltdowns and such. I was reminded of this a couple of weeks ago when I met a friend for lunch and a catch-up – we laughed and chatted and laughed some more, and when I got home I felt like a different woman. I realised that it had been weeks since I'd been out for something fun.

I'd seen friends, talked to them (briefly), and been in contact via social media, but I hadn't been out of the house for something fun. So when I did, it was something of a revelation. (I know, it's sad, but it's life for way too many of us.) We've replaced a social life with a social media life – in touch with friends for hours and hours. Trouble is our attention is split amongst 300 friends for those hours.

We're not getting quality friend time, or quality going out time, or quality relaxation time (if you haven't noticed it yet, internet-surfing for hours isn't that relaxing). We're getting what masquerades as downtime, but is actually filling up our heads with too much information, too many people and not enough LIFE. Real life. Where people converse and do things (not just read about them or see them on Instagram).

If you recognise yourself in this, I challenge you today to book some doing something in the real world time in the next week. You don't have to be out every night. I'm a hermitess, I have no intention of filling every spare second on my calendar with social stuff – it's exhausting (introvert-alert, that's how we feel about a lot of social stuff) and makes me ill.

On the other hand, I do need some time out in the real world doing stuff. Or I start bouncing off the walls, and that's no fun. So, switch off your tech and go hang out with some real people in a real place. Enjoy!

Don't let money, men, or jobs steal your joy

So you've got no money? This is no reason to lose your joy. So a bloke has been an asshat? This is no reason to lose your joy. So your job SUCKS? This is no reason to lose your joy.

"Remain cheerful, for nothing destructive can pierce through the solid wall of cheerfulness." – Sri Chinmoy, The Wings of Joy

I get it, I've been there. I've been so broke I've cried myself to sleep. I've been heartbroken, hurt and betrayed. I've been in jobs where I'd rather poke out my eyes with a dull knife than be there a minute longer. I've had bosses I couldn't describe even using every swear word possible in every language I know.

Just don't let them steal your joy. Ok, you can be momentarily worried or upset or motivated to leave. Just don't let them steal your joy. Don't let them undermine the good and the beautiful and the joyful in your life. Don't let them make your exquisite life awful.

We're human, so we're going to worry (until we learn not to); we're going to be sad; we're going to feel frustration and irritation. You don't have to live in a perpetual state of worry, sadness, frustration and irritation though. Many of us have got into a habit of allowing problems like no money, man trouble and crappy jobs to leech away our joy.

There is another choice. Live as joyously as you can, despite the money/men (or women)/jobs. Not only will you feel better, you'll be able to solve those problems more easily the lighter you feel. The more dark and down you are, the harder it is to sort out your money, to sort out your relationships, and to sort out your jobs.

The better you feel, the better you feel. The better you feel, the easier life is. Problems that seem insurmountable when we're unhappy become less significant the more joyful we are. And the truth is that up until now, you've survived all the money problems, man (or woman) problems, and lousy jobs.

Despite the times you were broke, heartbroken and worked at the Worst Job in the World, you're still going. For me, I always figured out the money stuff eventually, most of the men weren't worth the anguish and buckets of tears, and once I'd left the jobs, I never gave them another moment's thought.

I know it's easier said than done – we have worries, relationship pains, job dissatisfaction and they feel like a really big deal at the time. The more you can enjoy life anyway, outside of those issues, the better you will feel. So don't let money, men or jobs steal your joy.

Get rid of the things you don't enjoy

We all have things we do that we really don't enjoy doing. Some of them we have to do, some of them we think we have to do, some of them we don't have to do at all, we do because we're some kind of masochist. There are all sorts of reasons to do things we don't like to do, but often it's just because we haven't stopped to notice "hey, I really hate this" and made the decision to stop doing it.

Make a list of all the things you don't like doing, and get rid of the easiest thing to stop doing. If you hate ironing, get someone to do it for you, or do a swap with someone who hates polishing or shopping. If you hate going to action movies with the other half, tell them and let them find someone who won't sit there with a face like a spanked arse ruining the experience for them.

This brings me to a serious point. If you go along to something because you hate to let someone down, or because you can't say no, stop it. Yes, there are times when I just want someone to come with me (usually only if it's a last minute thing), but most of the time, I'd rather not spend half my time worrying that my friend isn't enjoying themselves.

You're not doing your friends a favour if you join them reluctantly, grudgingly, and miserably. You'll bring them down too. So tell them you don't like line-dancing or whatever and let them find someone else who will enjoy it, and make their experience even better. You'll also free up your time to do things YOU enjoy.

Of course, there will be things on your list that you cannot stop doing, like standing watching your son play football in the rain. For those things, try to find a way to make it more fun for you, or to do it a little less (alternate with another mom/dad). I've just got an image of little Johnny's disappointed little face that you're not on the sidelines.

Hey, sometimes when you don't want to, you've just got to suck it up for the sake of your loved ones, but do check, Little Johnny might secretly be glad that his mom's not standing on the sidelines with flat hair and running mascara embarrassing him by shouting "that's brilliant darling" when he's just given the ball away to the opposition.

Just sayin.

Anyway, if you don't enjoy it, don't do it. It doesn't make you a great person, it makes you a person who does stuff they don't enjoy. It's tough to fall in love with a life full of doing stuff you do not want to do. Often, you can shed enough of the stuff you don't like to make space for things you do like.

Sure, there's stuff you really do need to do that you might not like – attending hospital or dentist appointments for example. Don't be foolish about it; just dump a few of the things you can dump without endangering your health or devastating your loved ones. Take the time to notice 'wow, I really don't like this thing' and stop doing it.

Focus on what's good in your life, not what's wrong

It is so tempting to see only what needs fixing in our lives, because there's always something, right? Life's never perfect. We are never perfect. There's always something to change and improve and polish and correct and develop. So why not focus on that?

In short, because it makes us dissatisfied. You can see this most often with relationships. One, or both, partners focus on the things that are wrong with the relationship. Perhaps at the start to *improve* it, but eventually, it just becomes a habit to criticise and complain and moan.

After a while, friends of the couple wonder why the hell they're still together because they never have a good word to say, they always seem dissatisfied and unhappy (only not enough to break up and move on). I had a client in this situation, and I asked her to start focusing on what was good about her partner, to find things to compliment and to be nice. Just as an experiment.

She realised how on edge both of them had been because they were constantly expecting snippy little comments and bickering endlessly. Once they made an effort to behave like a couple who actually loved one another, they started to enjoy being together again.

You can try this with any of the people in your life – bosses, friends, significant others, shop workers – expecting the best of people, and treating them as if they're awesome often works wonders. I love being in a line of people with a really grumpy person dealing with the line – by the time I get to the front, I have a big smile all ready, I'm treating them as if they're the nicest person I ever met (unlike everyone else, who treats them like they're horrible, because that's what they've just seen).

90% of the time, they're lovely back to me. People live down to our expectations of them. So focus on what's good, be nice, be positive, treat them like a worthy, significant human being and they'll either live up to that, or they'll be who they are. Either way, you didn't contribute to them being a horrible person. Most people aren't.

You can see this in action with someone you know who is always complaining about bad service in restaurants. Watch how they treat their waitress. There's usually a direct correlation. Waitresses, shop workers, doormen are all people too – and usually nice, hard-working, good people who are often treated badly by people who think they're superior (they're clearly not, if they were they wouldn't need to be a jackass).

But if you treat these nice, hard-working, good people like they're inferior and stupid, they probably will be in response to you being horrible to them. I worked behind a bar from the age of 15, and I have seen all manner of rudeness, disrespect and disdain. It almost never made me respond with grace and my best work, I'm just not that big a person.

Life responds in the same way. If you're consistently concerned with every imperfection in your life, every area that needs improvement, every missing piece, you'll get into the habit of seeing only the bad and only feeling dissatisfied. I know this is pretty obvious, but feeling dissatisfied doesn't help you enjoy life. It has the opposite effect.

Your poor life is there, pretty pleased with itself for the fabulous things you have going on, and you're fault-finding and carping about one small thing. If you ignore all that's good about your life, you'll miss how good it really is. You'll go through life a disappointed malcontent and miss how good you really had it.

Some of us only realise this when we suffer a loss or a bad health diagnosis, or we lose what we had and then realise how lucky we were. I urge you not to do that. Notice what's great about your life and put more focus on that than on what sucks, what's missing, what's wrong. You can still fix any minor (or major) flaws in your life, but you can enjoy what's good in the meantime and change from a place of 'this is great, let's add this' instead of 'I hate my life'.

There's no point putting a happy face sticker on an empty petrol gauge

I've talked a lot about feeling good, about choosing to feel fabulous darling, about appreciation, about loving life. I also want to say don't pretend. Don't pretend to feel awesome when inside you're screaming. You're allowed to feel the full range of human emotion.

So often, we do not allow ourselves to feel how we feel – either because the emotion is a bad one, or because there's no point feeling joyful because it's Sunday and tomorrow we have work, or more regularly, we just don't have the time to feel how we feel.

So we swallow our anger, our fear, our irritation, our impatience, our hurt, our upset, our outrage, our pain. Even our delight, our joy, our love, our wonder at life don't get to be fully expressed too often – we even hold that in, not wanting to be embarrassed or appear childish or trying to look cool or some other excuse not to fully experience our joy.

Where does all this feeling go? Negative emotion, if it is not expressed, goes nowhere, it stays in our body, mind and heart; slowly poisoning us, making our heart hurt, making us want to scream over the sheer frustration of not being able to express ourselves. Sometimes this bursts out of us in a totally uncontrolled way as road-rage or trolley rage. Positive emotion, if unexpressed, smothers the joyful, playful inner child and we forget how to feel wonder, joy, playfulness, delight.

You're allowed to feel however you feel – good and bad. We can see the problems it causes when people don't allow themselves to feel how they feel (emotionally stunted exes anyone?). It's like putting a happy face sticker on an empty petrol gauge. There's still no fuel in the car. It still won't go, no matter how smiley and sparkly the sticker.

If you allow yourself to just feel how you feel and don't fight your feelings, you'll come to a point when you appreciate all of your feelings. You'll feel them, experience them, let them move through you and perhaps even enjoy them.

The first time I experienced this, I was observing myself be really cantankerous and snappy with my family. So I took myself away from them and enjoyed being bad-tempered by myself. (I hadn't been that grumpy for a while, it was kinda fun.)

I've also experienced it in grief. Not that I enjoyed feeling grief. I was asked by a coach at the time "why are you feeling so bad?", which I thought was the dumbest question ever, but I answered: "because I loved that person and they're gone". The depth of my love showed in the depth of my grief.

It's kind of a beautiful thing when you look at it that way. So although I can't say I had fun with the grief, I did appreciate it in a way. I appreciated what it showed me about the strength of my relationships with my dearly departed.

That's an extreme example. Most of the time, the emotions we're experiencing are not that deep and profound. Whether they're profound or trivial, they're your emotions. Don't deny them. Allow them, name them – notice you're feeling sad, angry, defeated, upset, peevish, fearful, irritated. Don't forget to notice the good emotions too – joy, love, happiness, delight etc.

Then allow them to move on, or if you're enjoying a positive emotion, luxuriate in it and intensify it and thoroughly enjoy it. When I'm feeling some negative emotion, I write it out, or dance it out, or walk it off, or talk it out, or sing "I'm not ok" at the top of my voice (PMT playlist) or in some cases I just sit with the feeling and stare at the wall with a sad face until it passes.

You feel how you feel, and that's allowed. Once you've felt it and moved it (or sat with it if that's what you need to do), you can make choices about what to feel next, how to be next, how to move your joy level up a touch, what to appreciate, what to be inspired by, how you'll refuel instead of ignoring the empty petrol gauge.

Part 7:

Dream teams and

Blueberries

Put your friends at the top of your priority list

You gotta have friends. More than that, you gotta make time to see and speak to those friends. Friends make you laugh, allow you to vent your frustrations, they support, encourage and celebrate your successes, and they bring the best out in you. If that's not worth making the time for, I don't know what is.

One of my goals for 2013 was to spend more time with friends, and not keep saying "oh we really should do this more often", but to actually DO this more often. It was a joy. It was so nice to see my closest friends more often, and not to spend half the day thinking 'we should do this more often'. All it takes is a bit of organisation.

Ok, there are still a couple of my friends I haven't seen in months or years because life stuff got in the way, but all it will take is for both of us to get our diaries out and set a date. It won't always work out, but there's a better chance if you have a date in the diary than if you don't.

If you don't arrange it, you'll think "we'll get together tomorrow" - and tomorrow never comes. Do it now. Get in touch with your bezzie and arrange a catch-up. Get in touch with a friend you wish you saw more of and arrange to see more of them. Get in touch with an old friend you haven't seen in 10 years and arrange a date to get together.

Don't let life get in the way. Yeah, you've got work and chores and family to take care of, and no time to see your friends. Make time. Do lunch, leave the ironing in favour of a night out with a friend, invite your friends round so you don't need a babysitter. Friends want to see you, they're not fussed about where. Rather than waiting 21 years 'til the kids are old enough, get your friends round. If they have kids, go to the park together.

Sometimes I am a complete hermit (usually in Winter) and I can go for weeks without seeing any of my friends – to the point that I forget I have friends and start singing "Nobody loves me, everybody hates me; I think I'm gonna eat worms". The truth is that I do have friends, I just haven't been in touch with them for a while.

In these busy times, it's far too easy to get isolated and feel alone when there's no need. Call your friends, arrange to see them, not just text or social media chat – online connection is great, but it's no substitute for real people. People you can laugh with and talk to and reminisce with and have fun with – your people. Put friend time at the top of your priority list today.

Teach other people how to treat you

Have you ever noticed that people who don't respect themselves don't tend to command respect? How people who are doormats get walked on? The truth is that we teach other people how to treat us. If we put our needs last, why would our family put our needs first? They learned from us that we can be put last.

It's not pretty, and if they were conscious of it, they'd possibly be a bit ashamed, but the buck has to stop with you. If you do not respect yourself, take care of your needs, treat yourself as important, the subliminal message you give out is that you're not worth it. When other people pick up on that, they won't treat you as well as you deserve.

I have had many a conversation about this that goes like this:

"They should just *know*."

"Why, are they psychic?"

"If they *loved* me they'd know what I want."

"Why don't you just tell them?"

Maybe it's my personality – I don't do well with waiting for someone to pick up that I'm ticked off with them, or need something. I prefer to just tell them. (Although they have to be pretty dense not to pick it up – what I feel is generally written all over my face.)

Being clear about my needs and irritations saves much upset on my part or confusion on the part of others. It makes life a lot easier when you're open and articulate about what you want. Even if you aren't entirely comfortable with saying "this is what I want" (Brits, as a rule, tend to suck at this), the better you treat yourself, the better other people will treat you.

In part, because you're setting the benchmark of care, and teaching them how to treat you by doing it yourself; and partly because when you are treating yourself like a Queen, you kick people who don't treat you well to the kerb.

There's another reason we need to model treating ourselves well – how can someone else be expected to take care of you when you don't really know what you want? Many of us have this vague feeling of dissatisfaction that we're not getting what we want from our loved ones, but when asked to articulate that, we're not clear ourselves.

Other people are not psychic. They don't have some magic window into your head to see that you being crotchety about the washing up is actually a sign that you feel taken for granted. Some people are more emotionally intelligent and might pick it up, but it's guesswork at best. So don't give your power away to someone else's speculation.

Treat yourself well, respect yourself, appreciate yourself. Show the people in your life what you deserve by living it. Start now, today. What do you need? Is it time out, a treat, a luxurious bath, some help with the chores, a laugh with a friend? Give it to yourself. Find a way to get that need met. Because you deserve the very best – and that starts with the way you treat yourself.

Your behaviour does teach the people around you, so make sure your behaviour is teaching them that you're a Queen, not a dogsbody. By the way, you don't need to be a tyrant Queen with your foot on the head of your loyal subjects. You can treat others well *as well as* treating yourself well – it's not an either or, it's a win/win.

Don't let ANYONE put you down

Sometimes people around us inadvertently put us down, sometimes they do it deliberately, but whether it's intended or not, don't accept it. You don't have to have a massive confrontation, you can just ignore it. (Although I do love a well-placed "who do you think you're talking to" or a clear "that's not a nice thing to say" to the offending individual.)

You can just refuse to take any notice of the put-down. My parents have a saying "Don't let the bastards grind you down" - and I love this advice. This is exactly what happens if you're not vigilant - years and years of criticism, digs, insults and unsupportiveness can just grind down your good humour and confidence. Don't let the bastards grind you down.

How do you stop them? Sometimes just saying something to the offender stops them, but often it doesn't, and changing other people is just such hard work. So here's what you can do: don't take it on. Don't give away your power to someone else. Don't allow other people to put you down. They can say the words, but if you don't listen, those words have no power alone. Words can be like acid, corroding and eating away at you; but not if you don't take it on.

Put it this way, if someone called you a blueberry, how much would you take that on board? How much would you allow that to hurt you? How much would you repeat it, worry about it, chew over it and keep hurting yourself with it? I am hoping you are saying 'not at all', because if someone called you a blueberry ...well, wtf?

But if they call us 'stupid' or they criticise and insult us with something more hurtful, that's exactly what we do - we take it as gospel, we allow ourselves to be hurt by it, we repeat it to ourselves and others and pick the scab off the hurt so much that we are scarred by it (and a thousand other little comments like it).

One person telling you that you are wrong does not make you wrong 100% of the time. One incident of being told you're a stupid, fat cow does not make it true. If you're the one repeating that one incident 200 times, who's the one hurting you?

So stop taking on this stuff - know yourself better, have confidence in yourself, and instead of repeating the bad stuff and giving it power, repeat this like a mantra: I am amazing, intelligent, worthy, wonderful and a really good laugh. If other people can't see that, that's their problem.

Include yourself in this too. You probably put yourself down fairly often. Most of us do, and we can be vicious with it. Most of us would never speak to anyone else the way we talk to ourselves (and if we did, we'd fully expect a punch in the mouth), so be vigilant - when I say don't let ANYONE put you down, I mean you too.

So if you need to, learn to talk to yourself like you're your best friend, biggest fan, most adoring suitor (I just got a brain-pic of Pepe-Le-Pew) and greatest cheerleader. Have that as your standard for the people around you too. "You're standing on my foot, get off" is acceptable; "you're a fat, lazy cow" is not.

You know the difference between a fair comment and a put-down. Learn to let the put-downs just wash straight off you, like water off a duck's back. Like someone just said "you sir, are a blueberry", and you thought "wtf?", and let it go. Because you are not a blueberry, or stupid, or worthless, or lazy, or whatever the insult is.

You are wonderful and beautiful and special. Don't let anyone tell you any different.

Spend more time with your happy people

Who are your happy people? Who are the people in whose company you feel safe and content and loved? Who are the people who make you laugh until your tummy hurts? Who are the people you love spending time with? How much time do you spend with those people?

When I looked at this, I found that I didn't spend that much time with friends that made me happy. One of my happiest friends, I saw about once a year. So, I made some changes. I didn't just cut all my other friends from my life; I just re-arranged my priorities a bit.

I started to make sure I spent more time with people who made me happy. Just doing that stopped me spending time with people who didn't, because I was busy having fun.

Don't panic if you find that the people you spend the most time with aren't your happy people. Just look for someone you love spending time with, see more of them, and you will naturally be more relaxed and a happier person yourself, and this will filter through to your other friends.

This activity might highlight where fun relationships have become moan-fests, or criticism-marathons, or bicker-fiestas. That's all to the good. Once you notice it, you can change it. It doesn't mean that you stop talking to your mother, divorce your husband or have a blazing row with your best friend of 38 years. It just means you are aiming to spend more time with people who make you happy.

And if you're going to spend a lot of time with your husband/mom/bezzie, then give some thought to making that time happy time – do things you both enjoy, reminisce about happy memories, laugh together. Sometimes stressful times in our lives change us from happy, cheerful, fun people to stressed out, gloomy, grumps.

I am not suggesting that you drop friends who are having a hard time, or that you should enter a monastery if you are going through a rough time. Friends stick together through good times and bad.

However, the more time you spend with people who make you happy, the more cheerful you will be, and the more you will spread sunshine in the world.

A client of mine found that she always felt exhausted and fed up after going out with her main group of friends. She started to see more of other friends who made her laugh and were light and happy (even though one of them was having treatment for breast cancer, she was still mostly a ray of sunshine).

Her energy rose, her level of enjoyment of life rose, she started to work on dreams she'd held in her heart for years; and the other group? Well, she started to spend time with them individually and found that most of them were happy friends - but as a group, they tended to be catty and moany. So other than one woman my client had not been close to anyway, she kept all her friends, she just saw them in a different way.

Notice the impact that the people you spend time with have on you, and make more time for the people whose impact is positive. If some of your friendships have got into a bit of a moany rut, make the effort to be the change – be the cheerful, fun one. Be the person who brings sunshine to the table - it's infectious, so your friends will catch it too and become happy friends.

Don't try to change others

So, I guess, like me, that you KNOW that if only the world would do as you tell it to, it would be a perfect place, right? Never mind the fact that the attitude is a wee bit dictatorish, and I know that you are a lovely person. If other people would just behave the way you think they should, your life would be perfect.

However, those pesky other people think the same thing. If only you'd behave in a way that is acceptable to them, their life would be perfect. I suspect, like me, you have no intention of living your one and only life according to someone else's rules. So why on earth would you expect them to live to your rules?

When I share this particular idea with clients we always have a version of this argument:

"Yes, but they should just xyz."

"Perhaps. But do they?"

"No, but if they did that would solve the problem"

"Perhaps. But will they?"

"No, but if they did…"

"And the reality is…?"
"Well, that's beside the point, what they should do is…"
"And back in the real world…"

The conversation normally lasts a good 15 minutes. I understand entirely. If my loved ones would just behave as I wish, life would be a far more orderly place. They won't. They will carry on doing what they do, living their life, being themselves, expressing their personalities, dealing with things in their own way.

When I think about it, I prefer it that way. Not only do I have no intention of living by someone else's rules, I think it would be a bit weird and creepy if they lived to mine (as all my loved ones are independent, unique types). Plus, I am too lazy and too nice to be a dictator. You need a lot more psychopath points than I'm prepared to get.

It's a lot of effort to try to change other people, usually completely futile effort. Most of the time we just carp about wanting them to change, and they don't. So you have a choice. You can either keep running uphill through treacle with steel boots on, and a blindfold, while being shot at by snipers (metaphorically), or you can stop it.

Let other people be who they are, don't try and make them be how you think they should be. They won't. It's a waste of precious energy. All the time you spend in their business, you're not in your own business. Get your own house in order. Ironically, people often do change when you stop trying to force the issue – try it, you might be amazed.

"Do not seek to straighten another
Do a harder thing instead-
Straighten yourself"
- Buddha teachings on relationships

This doesn't just apply to your loved ones by the way – you may want to relieve yourself of the stress of disagreeing vociferously and passionately with anyone. For one thing, it rarely changes their opinion. Arguing generally just entrenches people in their own point of view. I know when someone starts arguing with me, it isn't the quickest way to change my mind.

Arguing with me just gets me to argue back. It doesn't change my opinion, because I'm too busy defending my position in the argument. It's a waste of breath. Sometimes it's totally ok to let both of you be right – the best band/sports team/food is totally subjective and matters not a jot. We all have different opinions and ideas and that is as it should be – variety is the spice of life and all that.

Does this mean you let people get away with being jackasses? Certainly not. You can still let them know they're being a jackass; just stop wasting your time trying to make them be different. I remember a conversation with a misogynistic, racist fool where he expected me to respond as a shrill feminist bleeding heart – he had all his arguments ready.

I decided he wasn't worth the breath to argue with, just said 'I disagree' and changed the subject. In the end, we had quite an interesting conversation about race and gender; and although I disagreed with almost everything he said, I believe he actually heard a couple of my points. I'm sure it didn't change him overall, but I'm also sure it was one of the few times he'd actually heard what a woman had to say.

You know me, it's about what works, not how the world should work. Keep your energy in your own life, and show people by example what changes they could make, or just agree to disagree.

You don't have to be superwoman

Everyone has bad days. Let me say that again. EVERYONE has bad days. Yes, some people will deal with them more easily than others, and that's what we want to do, just get better and better at the business of life. None of us can do that alone. We need support. We need help. We need people to be vulnerable with us and let us be vulnerable too.

I am surprised at how often I hear the question "is it just me?" Is it just me who feels vulnerable? Is it just me who gets scared? Is it just me who is having a wobble? Is it just me who has struggles? Is it just me who wonders if it'll ever happen for me? Nope, nope, nope. It's not just you. Everyone has times when they feel vulnerable, or afraid, or they wobble, or struggle, or lose faith. Everyone.

The trouble is, so many of us go around pretending to be superwoman, putting on the public face, the stiff upper lip, when inside we are screaming and in desperate need of help. Well, it's time to stop this absurd way of living. You're human. You're allowed to feel vulnerable when you do something new and scary. You're allowed to feel fear. You're allowed to mess up - mightily if you so choose. You're allowed to experience the full range of what it means to be human.

If you go through life pretending to be superwoman, you miss out on the joy that comes with sharing a confidence and having a friend say "yeah, me too". You miss out on the relief of expressing your inner experience, and you miss out on the wealth of wisdom that exists on how to get past whatever you're experiencing. Of course, you don't want to stay in the vulnerable, fearful place, but you can move past it much quicker if you share and ask for help, or just share and give help.

Because if you insist on only showing your best face to the world, you're part of the problem. The problem that has people wondering if it's just them because you don't allow them to see any chinks in your armour. The wolves won't turn on you if you show vulnerability and most people LOVE to help and support others, so you're giving them a chance to do so.

Oh, and PS, in the spirit of showing behind the curtain, I haven't always practised what I'm preaching here. In 2012 I had a big wobble and didn't reach out for help, so my friend told me she'd beat me up if I did it again. Sometimes all you need is a little incentive to reach out for help. There's mine.

As well as your friends and family, there is also a circle of professional supporters – coaches, therapists, body workers, consultants. Get the professional support you need too. I had always been of the mind that I should be able to do it all myself, but last year I realised that I couldn't do it all alone, I never had done it all alone, and my stubborn insistence that I should be able to do it all alone was actually getting in the way of my business being successful and my life being joyful.

Get over any pride you have, and get the help you need.

Create your dream team

Let's take the idea of not being superwoman a little step further, and create a Dream Team around you to help you live and love your life. It makes the journey faster, easier and more fun if you create your Dream Team. I am one of the worst people in the world for trying to do it all by myself. I am very independent and self-sufficient, which most of the time is a positive thing, but sometimes it is an Achilles heel.

Doing it alone means missing out on support – what you need most when you're having a wobble. Doing it alone means missing out on experience – which could save you years of heartache and frustration. Doing it alone means your blind spots become your weakest spots – which can really get in your way. If there's no one around to point out that you are banging your head against a brick wall, you will end up with one hell of a headache.

Get support, get help, get your Dream Team around you. Let people in, let them help and support you – all the time. Educate them about how to do that. If what you need is a morale boost, say so. If what you need is sympathy, say so. If what you need is a giant kick up the bum, say so. If what you need is honesty, say so.

A good Dream Team can make a huge difference to you loving life and making your dreams come true. At the Oscars, you never hear an acceptance speech that says "thanks to me and only me, cos I'm just flipping brilliant". If someone did that, they would probably have to run the gauntlet of hundreds of livid friends and colleagues who helped them get to that Oscar.

You don't have to do it alone, but you don't have to do it with a default support team of your family and neighbours. People all have different skills and gifts. Some are amazing at finding the perfect shoe to complete the outfit. Some are wonderful at cheering you up. Some are fantastic at bitching with you about how much life sucks and what an asshat your boss is. Some will smack you upside the head and tell you to get a new job.

You get to choose who you put on your Dream Team. This doesn't necessarily mean cutting people off entirely – it might mean spending a little less time with them, setting rules, or re-educating them on how you want to be supported in your life. If you can train a dog to beg, roll over, fetch and sit, you can teach a person to support you in the way you want them to.

Just like dogs, humans respond better to positive reinforcement than telling them off all the time – and they're much less likely to bite you if you train nicely.

There are some really great people out there in the world, just waiting to help you enjoy your life to the fullest – go find them. And those people already in your life? Let them in, let them help, let them be your supporter, your cheerleader, your shoulder to cry on, your friend to belly-laugh with, your dream team.

Be ELSIE (encouraging, loving, supportive, inspiring and empowering)

There is an interesting phenomenon in the world today – the media spend a lot of their time tearing people down, criticising and reporting that "shock! Horror! This person is human." Like, omg, really? That celeb/politician/businessperson is not perfect? Hold my hat while I stand back in amazement.

I'm not talking here about reporting fraudulent, illegal or immoral behaviour – that use of media I understand and support. It's the media that reports every minor flaw in anyone's appearance or personality I'm talking about here. You can see it on a smaller level when we gossip and criticise and bad-mouth various people.

It's seen as a fairly harmless hobby, but it can be crushing to us and to the people we love. Because subconsciously if we hear that it is not safe to poke our head over the parapet, we'll be too afraid of getting shot at to go for a different life. This may sound a bit hyperbolic, but trust me – almost every client I work with has some fear around sticking their neck out to do something new and this didn't come from nowhere.

It came from cultural norms of criticism, discouragement, negativity and judgement. From a culture that encourages and supports bitchiness. The good news is that if we change the cultural norm in a small way in our own lives, this helps not only us feel more able to step up and live the life we were born to live (the most joyful feeling in the world), but it also helps the people around us to do the same.

Think of your partner, your best friend, your children - do you want them to be too afraid to step up and live their best life? Or do you want them to have the confidence to go live the life they really want to live? If the latter, then be encouraging, loving, supportive, inspiring and empowering.

Be the voice that says 'you can do it', the voice that says 'I believe in you'. Be the support when your loved ones lose faith in themselves. Love on your loved ones, even when they're being imperfect (real). Inspire them with positive stories and ideas. Empower your people – believe in them, trust them, back them up, be their biggest cheerleaders.

All this is a coach's job, but we shouldn't be the only ones who get the joy and the fun and the exhilaration from encouraging, supporting, loving, inspiring and empowering people. It's so much fun to be a building block in someone's success, instead of one of the (too many) boots trying to kick down their walls. So make the effort to rise above the petty, critical, cynical, nasty, mean behaviour and be ELSIE.

Wait! Don't only be it, **accept it** from your people too. You may even want to limit the time you spend with people who are discouraging, unsupportive, critical and undermining. After all, you want to fall in love with your life – and to do so, you probably need to make some changes. To do that you will probably need encouragement, support, love, inspiration and empowerment. Right?

Receive generously

How are you at receiving? Do you graciously say "thank you, that is most kind" or do you say "no, no, I'm fine, thank you, no" whenever anyone offers you anything? Do you graciously say "thank you, I appreciate that" when you are given a compliment, or do you rebut the compliment with some dismissive comment?

For some reason, we have got the notion from somewhere that it is good to give, bad to receive. But if no one received, no one would be able to give. There's a circle of life thing going on here – give – receive – give – receive. Without the receiving bit, it all falls apart and you have friends arguing in a coffee shop over who is going to pay.

I have friends who find it very difficult to receive, and my failsafe way to give to them is to make it very clear that I shall be hurt and offended if they refuse. Or I just insist. It would be easier if they could just receive. I get it, I still don't always find it easy to receive. Sometimes I have to clamp my mouth shut so I don't say "no, no, I'll get it", and sometimes it's only afterwards I realise I've been ungracious.

Two things changed my ability to receive: One, someone told me that refusing a compliment was like throwing a gift back in someone's face. Ouch. That would be terribly rude and I'm frightfully British so I decided to learn to receive compliments. (Top tip: Just say thank you. It's all that's needed, then clamp your mouth shut.) Secondly, I realised how much I enjoy giving and to deny my friends that joy seemed churlish, rude and disagreeable.

Think about it – when you can easily give to and make a difference to their life, isn't it a joyful experience? Why wouldn't you want to give that to them? Why wouldn't you want to allow them to treat you? Why wouldn't you give them the pleasure of being generous?

There are of course reasons to do with self-esteem and worthiness, but frankly, you need to get over yourself – it's the generous thing to do to receive from people you love and respect. We all love to give, so let us give. Be generous to your friends and family and allow them to be generous to you.

Of course it's not good to take advantage of people and constantly take, take, take; but honestly, if you're even a little worried about that, you probably aren't a taker. Takers wouldn't worry about it.

This is also not about taking from people who want something back from you (this is not generosity, it's bribery) – especially if you do not want to pay the price for their generosity. It's perfectly ok to refuse that, but don't refuse the genuine generosity of people who love you and want to give to you with no expectation of return.

Don't give your power away to OPO's

OPO's – other people's opinions – can be a plague. Whether you ask for them or not, other people's opinions will invade your psyche, make you doubt yourself, pull you this way then that way, and perhaps even drive you a bit loopy. But other people's opinions are just that - THEIRS. You don't have to like or agree with them, they don't have to like or agree with your opinions.

"I don't care what you think of me. I don't think about you at all." Coco Chanel.

I adore this quote – it's so strong, feisty, powerful and courageous. It says 'this is MY life and what you think of it is entirely your business, not mine'. It says 'butt out bud'. It's a good one to remember when someone is pontificating about your life, or criticising you. It's your life, it's none of their business.

It works the other way round too – what you think about someone else's life is your business, not theirs. They don't have to listen (and most often, they don't). This is great news. It means you can stay in your business without taking on their opinions unless you want to.

I've been in business for over a decade now, and I know that people – friends, neighbours, acquaintances, random people who don't even actually know me – have judged me. Judged my choices. Judged my progress, my success, my methods, my path, my output, my bank account.

Some people judge me harshly and think I've made poor choices. Some people judge me crazy and stubborn and believed I should have given up in the early years. Some people think I'm brave and tenacious and smart and made great choices. Some of these opinions (the good and the bad), I agree with. Some of them I disagree completely with (the good and the bad).

Ultimately, the only person with the information to make a judgement on my life, my business, my choices and so on, is me. Even my perspective is skewed – depending on the day, the time in my cycle and how things are going, I'm either a business genius or a blithering idiot who should just get a proper job where they pay you holiday and sick and tell you what to do and you get bank holidays and weekends and evenings off.

See, that's how crazy judgement is. On any given day, it's just an opinion about something most people don't have the complete facts on. That opinion isn't gospel. Even the people you most admire and respect may have opinions that just don't connect with the knowledge in your heart. You're the expert on your life. You're the one who knows what you'll do; never mind what everyone else thinks about it.

I have always been a little bit contrary. When everyone thought I should stay at uni, I came home and had a year out (I spent 6 months unemployed and 6 months in a lousy job and went galloping back to uni as if my tail was on fire the following year). I just knew I had to take a year out, even though OPO's were telling me not to do it.

When most people I knew thought I should use my savings to put down a deposit on a house, I blew it on a trip to the other side of the world. It's not that OPO's mean nothing to me; it's just that I don't give the reins of my life to other people – especially those who don't know me. I know that their opinions count a lot less than my own. Because it's my life. I spend as little time as I can thinking about what everyone else thinks about how I live my life.

"Don't worry about hurting my feelings because I guarantee you not one bit of my self-esteem is tied up in your acceptance" – Dr Phil

Honestly, I'm not quite there with Dr Phil yet, it is still possible to hurt my feelings – but I'm working on it. If you can unhook your self-esteem from the opinions of other people – whoever they are, you will gain the freedom to live your life to your rules with no fear. Worth thinking about, isn't it?

Part 8:

The Wheel of Life

Get shit in perspective

Having lost several people very dear to me in my lifetime, I know all about the really truly dreadful, heart-wrenching, painful, awful things that can happen in life. I know about the depression and the lethargy that comes with deep grief. I've lived through some hard and horrible times. As have we all.

In a lifetime, we go through some truly distressing and difficult times. Compared to them, most of the day to day tripe is a grain of sand in the desert – insignificant and unimportant in the grand scheme of things. Yet we let those day to day, petty, unimportant things bother us.

The dictionary defines perspective as "a way of regarding situations, facts, etc., and judging their relative importance". When we get things totally out of perspective, we over-react, get stressed, fly off the handle, bend the ears of our poor put upon loved ones, and so on. Over things that in a week or a month or a year we won't remember, let alone care about.

Of course, this is going to happen. I'm not asking you to be a robot. It is human to react. It is normal. I am asking you to make it less and less normal. Get things in perspective. Judge their relative importance. The day to day stuff, the arguments with your boss, the disappointments, the unexpected bills - compared to the worst days of your life so far, these mean nothing.

Sometimes it takes something God-awful happening in your life to remind you how unimportant most things are. When I have lost friends and family, the day to day shiz that seemed so significant the day before meant absolutely nothing, I couldn't have cared a toss.

One day I was worried about where my business would go and what I would do next, the next you could have destroyed my business with a rocket and I wouldn't have given a monkey's. Compared to losing my loved ones, it didn't matter one bit. You don't have to wait until terrible things happen to get perspective. You can get it today.

Take one thing that's bothering you. Will you remember it in a week? In a month? In a year? If not, don't worry about it. Get it in perspective. Breathe, and let it go. This does not mean you don't sort out the things that are bothering you – if you can do something about a situation that's bugging you, do it - just without the stress and drama.

We all know drama Queens – I've been known to be a bit of a drama Queen myself – and they have a hard life. Everything is such a big deal, such a tragedy, such a scene. That's a very stressful way to live. When everything is either life or death, that's hard on the blood pressure. It's usually not life or death (unless you happen to be a doctor, nurse or paramedic). Often it's not even that memorable.

I remember talking to a client once about the *worst day of her life* at work where her boss had been being a jerk. We got it in perspective and she was shocked at how significant she'd made it, at how wound up she got over something that really didn't mean anything. He was a jerk that day, that was it. It didn't even affect her work.

Like I say, we're human, it happens. If you can train yourself to take a breath and remember that most of the things you worry about aren't that significant, your blood pressure and your life will be happier.

Don't borrow trouble from tomorrow

How much time and energy do you waste on worrying about things that never happen? I know for me, it's too much time. Time and energy that if I wasn't worrying, I could be doing something far more constructive. I saw a statistic somewhere that over 80% of the things we worry about never happen. Personally, I think it's more like over 90%. How about you?

When we worry, we're borrowing trouble off tomorrow. Trouble we don't need today, because today has its own troubles. Plus, it doesn't help. Worrying doesn't help you feel better about a situation, it makes you feel worse. Worrying doesn't help you deal with a situation, it makes you anxious, interrupts your sleep, and drives you slightly crazy. All of which actually hinder your ability to deal with a situation.

The endless what-ifs and dark scenarios of death, bankruptcy and job loss (amongst other worries) aren't helping you in any way to make your life better. On the other hand, borrowing trouble from tomorrow does help to make your life worse. Spending time in that round and round and round place of 'what if?' and 'then if' and 'omg then if' is exhausting, makes you restless and afraid and can turn you into a basket case.

I don't know about you, but turning into a basket case isn't one of my top 100 desires in life. So how do you stop worrying? How do you stop borrowing trouble from tomorrow? It's easy to say 'stop it', and ultimately, that's what you need to do, but maybe you need a little more than that? So, here it is:

Trust yourself to deal with whatever comes up.

Because you will deal with it. You always have. Even the things that were unimaginably bad that you could never imagine dealing with – deaths too early of loved ones, job losses, relationship break ups, financial messes. You've dealt with them all so far. Because you do. That's life. You deal with it. You cope. You manage. You figure it out.

Let me share a conversation I had with one of my best friends before I left for Australia:

"Have you heard from K?" (K is the person who was picking me up from the airport.)

"No, but she knows my flight details."

"What if she's not there?"

Shrugs "I'll figure something out."

"Ok, it's 4 am, you're the other side of the world with nowhere to go and you don't know anyone, WHAT ARE YOU GOING TO DO?"

Laughs "I'll figure it out."

This conversation drove my poor friend wild. I can see why, I just didn't see the point in worrying about it days in advance. Honestly, I was a little more prepared than this conversation suggests. I had thought about it, and if K hadn't turned up, I'd have found a hotel. They have them in Australia. It would have been fine. I'd have figured it out.

As it turned out, the lovely K was there to get me and I didn't need to worry about it. (However, I did arrive in several cities in Australia with nowhere to go and no one I knew. Each time I figured it out.) So all that energy my friend put into stressing out about me was utterly wasted. (Or maybe not, if you consider this tale a useful example.)

There's no harm in having a contingency plan, in running through some ideas about what you might do if… But ultimately until it happens, you won't know what you'll do. I always had the contingency plan of a temp job if ever I couldn't pay my bills via my business. As it turned out, I didn't use it. I hustled and got more business instead.

You know the difference between contingency planning and worrying, right? One feels good and helps you feel more relaxed and at ease. The other stresses you out, gives you a headache and makes you feel a bit sick. I know how much you love to worry and how you'll miss it when it's gone, but just try not worrying on for size.

Stop borrowing trouble off tomorrow, and whenever you find yourself mithering, remind yourself you'll figure it out, you'll deal with it. Because you are endlessly capable, inspiringly strong, and a creative genius. So there's no problem life can throw at you that you can't overcome.

Let go of past crap

Imagine every bad experience you ever had has been packed into a suitcase for you (it might be a really BIG suitcase), and you are dutifully dragging that thing around with you everywhere you go. It slows you down, it gives you backache, it gets caught on stuff – walls, trees, cars; it knocks over random people in your path. And you could just put it down and carry on your merry way without it.

Doesn't that sound even a little bit appealing? Just to let go of that heavy, battered, old suitcase full of junk you don't even want anymore? You can't erase the past, you can't go back and change it (yet – I have high hopes that the DeLorean will still become a time machine), but you can let go of rubbish you don't need to carry around forever.

Some experiences aren't easily released – traumatic, horrific events are not easy to let go of alone – we need help to get rid of their hold on us. So if you have traumatic and horrific events in your past, I urge you to get help to process and release them. For most of us, it's just the accumulated clutter of a lifetime of experience of loss and pain and fear and irritations and idiots.

What we then do is lock it up tight in that suitcase. We might never think about it, but it's there. We might not even think it affects us anymore, but our response to a similar situation is clouded by that past event. If you have a cheating ex in your suitcase (now isn't that a lovely image?), you're more likely to be suspicious of new people, even if they give you no cause for suspicion.

That's why you need to let them out of the suitcase and let them go. Past hurts, past regrets, past sorrow and failure. Let them go. Don't lock them up tight in your suitcase. When I was young I had my heart broken a couple of times in a row, and I locked my heart up tighter than a miser's purse. What I didn't realise at the time was that I wasn't just locking out future possibilities, I was locking in the old heartbreak.

It was only when I started opening up my heart again, I realised I had locked a lot of the old pain and resentment in there, and it had years to fester. Bleurgh. So many of us do that. We swallow down our hurts, we close our hearts, we gird our loins, we pull ourselves up by our bootstraps, put the hurt in the suitcase and try to carry on; while simultaneously dragging that damn suitcase around with us.

So maybe it's time to let it go? Maybe it's time to release old hurts (like balloons released to the sky), to leave the suitcase behind (you can always come back and pick it up if you miss dragging it around), to let go of the past. It happened, and unless Marty McFly appears with a time machine it's not going to unhappen. Let it go.

Have you seen the Lion King? When Rafiki hits Simba over the head with a stick? (Search on YouTube if you've never seen it.) Simba says "Ow. What did you do that for?" Rafiki replies "it doesn't matter, it's in the past". What's in your past that no longer really matters? Is it time to stop dragging it around with you?

This can be as easy as making a decision to let it go, quit picking the scab and stop talking about it, or it can require therapy, time and repeated release (that blasted suitcase sometimes seems to be following you about, but the truth is you pick it up again without even noticing). Whatever help you need to let go of past crap, get it.

Old bosses and boyfriends that enraged you. Let them go – they've influenced your life long enough. Irritations about things people *always* do. Let it go, it doesn't matter. Old betrayals that felt so significant at the time, but now really don't matter at all. Let them go. Old stories of how you were done wrong by people you no longer care about. Let it go. That suitcase is heavy, and you don't need it. Let it go.

Stop trying to do 100 things at once

Single-tasking. Have you ever heard of it? It's when you do one thing at a time – you give your full attention to whatever you're doing, instead of trying to do everything all at the same time, and constantly wandering into rooms of your house (or open windows on your computer) and finding a half-finished task you'd forgotten about.

Single task is one of my life rules. It's a rule I break fairly often, but it's also the rule that I know helps me keep my sanity. I used to always have at least 10 windows open on my PC, and it would take me over an hour to close down at night because I had to finish 7 things I'd started during the day. Now, I have 4 windows open – this one, my internet browser with my thesaurus at the ready, my progress spreadsheet so I can geek out and add chapters and hours spent to it as I go, and a music app.

All of them are relevant to what I'm working on right now, as opposed to having 7 different projects open at once (plus Facebook and Twitter and Pinterest - just in case I wanted to skive). It feels so much better, life is so much easier, and I am a lot calmer. Now if I decide to finish work, it'll take me 5 minutes to shut down instead of 5 hours.

I'm a convert to single tasking. In my experience, multi-tasking is inefficient (getting nothing done on seven projects vs getting something done on one, anyone?), it overtaxes your brain and makes you stressed. It might look good (to those who wear their stress like a badge of honour), but it neither feels good nor works well.

If you've ever had (or tried to have) a conversation with someone while they're also on their phone texting or checking twitter, it's rude. Some things, of course, can be done together – like writing and listening to music (Rihanna is currently singing about diamonds as I write this) or ironing while watching TV, but mostly, single-tasking is the way forward.

Try it. You might be surprised at how much you can get done when you're not trying to do 100 things at once.

Don't give up

I've lost count of the number of times a client has said to me "I've tried EVERYTHING" (top tip: don't say this to your coach until you have at least 10 things you've done to back up the statement). When I ask what they've done, they list one, occasionally two things they've tried.

Hmm. Trying one or two things is not *everything*. It's not even *many* things. Trying one or two things to solve a problem is a start. Why not try five or six things, maybe even ten or twelve things? When you try a solution and it doesn't work, evaluate why to get a better idea about what to try next, and keep trying until the problem gets solved.

You don't need to bang your head against a brick wall – if something isn't working, evaluate and *change* it. Sometimes making a choice not to do something is a good choice. As long as it is a choice, not a surrender, not saying 'oh, what's the point, I've tried *everything* (2 things) and *nothing* (of the 2 things) worked' – there's a big difference between choosing something different and giving up.

You don't need to become a total pain in the backside either – nagging and going on about an issue doesn't often solve it. Get your creative hat on and think: What exactly is the problem? What ideas do you have to solve it? Who else do you know who has solved a similar problem? What did they do?

Can you get help? When Plan A fails, what's plan B, C, D, ZZ? It's so tempting to think 'I tried, I can't fix it/do it/change it, I give up', but please don't do that. Mostly because doing nothing is definitely not going to solve the problem. I remember having a conversation with my yoga teacher a few years ago about Plan Z (as in Plan A, Plan B, all the way to Z), and she said: "You're a terrier, not everyone is like that".

I wasn't always a terrier. I was a giveuper. When I worked in the corporate world, I would try everything (one or two things) and then give up. Because what's the point? I can't change X. Since I've had my own business, I've realised just how tenacious and determined I am (some would call it "stubborn as a herd of mules").

Perhaps it's because I'm a coach. It's my job to find ways round, over, under and through obstacles. It's my job to help people take responsibility for their own lives and experiences. It's my job to help people to stop feeling powerless and get out Plans A-Z. I get to help people to brainstorm ways to solve a problem, suggest new ways to look at situations and make life better and better in a thousand ways.

It's my default thinking 'ok, that didn't work, now what can we try?' For some of us, the default thinking is 'that didn't work. The end.' Tenacity and determination are learnable skills – I learned them. I went from 'what's the point?' to 'what's next?' in just a few short years.

Just in case you're curious, the point is this: if you keep trying you might just change things. Even if you don't, you'll know that you tried everything you could think of. You'll have built up muscles of tenacity and determination. You'll feel less at the mercy of a capricious life. Even if you don't succeed in the end, trying feels good.

These obstacles and blockages that come up in life are not there to stop you. They're there to help you to clear things that aren't working for you, or to build new muscles, or to flex your creative talents, or to step into your power, or to develop skills and talents you never anticipated needing, or to expand your capacity to ask for help.

Just as I was writing this, I wandered away to Facebook for a second (I do that – I have the attention span of a gnat) and found this on a motivational poster *"I will never truly fail because I will never stop trying"*. We are often in situations where we feel powerless and unable to change a thing. Sometimes that is genuinely true. However, more often, there is something you can do, something else you can try. Sometimes all you need is a different perspective to see another potential solution. Just don't give up.

Paddle your own canoe

This, darling heart, is your life. Who is paddling the canoe? Is it you? Your family? Your friends? Society at large? The Government? If anyone but you is paddling your canoe, snatch the paddle out of their hands and whack them upside the head with it.

It's your life. Your canoe, as it were. You need to paddle it yourself. You need to take control. Make your own choices. Be your own authority. Live your life. Don't blame anyone else for where your life is at (or yourself – what is past is past), get in your canoe and paddle to where you want to be.

By the way, this doesn't always mean frantically going OCD about steering your canoe in the perfect direction – that will just drive you crazy. Furthermore, if you just keep your head down and paddle frantically, you'll miss some great moments and maybe a couple of signposts saying 'fabulous stuff this way'.

Some days you'll be running the rapids, praying you don't hit a rock and sink your canoe. Some days you'll sit and watch the scenery roll by while you sit back with the sun on your face and let the current take you. Other days you'll be manoeuvring your canoe to catch a faster current, or exploring a tributary that catches your attention.

The direction of your canoe (your life) is up to you. The speed you go is up to you. Whether you get stuck on sandbanks, that's up to you too. Getting off the blasted sandbanks, also down to you. You can use the current, you can paddle your own canoe in a relaxed, laid back, easy going kind of way. Paddle in the general direction of stuff you want and see what the river of life brings you along the way.

This also means keeping your nose out of what's going on in all the other canoes – if you've got your paddle in someone else's canoe, who's steering yours? Of course, you will help your friends and family in their lives, but you help them most by setting a good example. Not by sitting primly, never swearing and being the perfect Stepford weirdo, but by living your life to the fullest, whatever that means to you.

By having the courage to paddle your own canoe – and decorate that canoe bright bookworm or full-on nerd, if that's what works for you. By keeping the optimism and naivety of youth, and knowing that you have years in front of you to figure out how to paddle this canoe where you want it to go, to explore your world and to experience every bit of that river of life.

The wheel of life takes you high and low

One of my favourite authors is Philippa Gregory, a historical novelist who writes about the English court in the heady days of Henry VIII and co. In several of her novels, she features a character called Elizabeth Woodville, who says "The wheel of life takes you high and it takes you low", which feels to me like a perfect way to end this book.

Life isn't all highs or all lows. It's a mix of good and bad, joy and sorrow, excitement and boredom, love and loathing, ups and downs. That is just life. Sometimes we're on the top of the wheel looking over the world like a Queen. Sometimes we're just trying to get through the next day, praying that no other shit can fall on us.

The wheel of life takes you high and it takes you low. Your job is to deal with the highs and the lows in the best way you can, to wring the most enjoyment you can from it all.

I got some of the best laughs of my life out of the house I lived in as a student, in one of the coldest places in England, with gaps under the door you could limbo dance under. It was the worst place I've ever lived (and the worst place I ever hope to live), but we had some laughs. We made the best of a god-awful situation which made us all ill and slightly psychotic.

If you can make falling in love with life one of your top priorities, you can ride the lows more easily – with grace and humour and peace and harmony. And you can enjoy the highs even more when they come because you're feeling great anyway, so good times are an added bonus.

The wheel of life will take you high and take you low, but whether you're high or low right now, I encourage you to delight in life anyway. I encourage you to approach it all as a grand adventure that you get to dance through – sometimes the dance will be chaotic – you'll be a whirling dervish of colour and laughter. Sometimes the dance will be slow, holding those you love close while you feel the tears on your face.

Keep dancing anyway. Let life take you where it will while you squeeze any joy you can from whatever gets thrown at you. Never forget that joy lies in the smallest of moments – in a ray of sunshine, in a piece of music, in a shooting star, in a smile from a loved one (or a complete stranger), in a moment to breathe, in a snuggle under the duvet moment, in a flower, in a memory. These things are always available, no matter how horrible the outer circumstances.

"I finally figured out the only reason to be alive is to enjoy it."
— Rita Mae Brown.

I couldn't have said it better myself. I wish you all the joy in the world in your life. I wish you love and light and happiness and laughter. I wish for you to fall head over heels in love with your wonderful life. I wish for you to realise what a beautiful soul you are. I wish for you to live all the days of your life with a smile in your heart and your dancing shoes on

.

Final thoughts

Note from the Author

I truly hope that you have enjoyed this book and started to fall more in love with your wonderful life. If you have enjoyed it, please feel free to share it. Tell all your friends about it. Shout it from the rooftops and on Facebook and Twitter. Come over to my facebook page (facebook.com/donnaonthebeach) and tell me which tip hit the mark most for you. You'll also find weekly Fall in Love With Life tips there using the doodles from the book (plus some new ones I've come up with since the book came out).

Come over to www.donnaonthebeach.com and join my list for free weekly love your life tips as well as to be the first to know about new releases and projects.

This book has been through many edits, with several people, and even several software programs, but nothing is infallible and you might have caught an error or spelling mistake…if you did, I'd be very grateful if you'd let me know. Spelling and grammar mistakes make me twitch and yet, some always seem to slip through the net, so if you spot one, come to donnaonthebeach.com to let me know, or you can find me under 'Donnaonthebeach' on Facebook and Twitter.

(Please note, I'm British, so if you're elsewhere in the world, you may spell things a little differently to me.)

And of course, if you have a spare minute, leave me a review on your favourite book retailer. I'll love you forever if you do.

Love
Donna ♡

About the Author

I work with women (and a few men) who *know* there is more to life; I help them to fall in love with their lives, find their deepest dreams and make them a reality. My deepest dream is to have the freedom to follow my inspiration every day (and to spend more time by the sea than I get to now). You will find me in the centre of England surrounded by paper, pens, books and Kindles.

Come on over to www.donnaonthebeach.com to find out more about how you can work with me to fall in love with your life and make your Big Dreams a reality. You will also find more articles, products, and fabulous freebies to help you make the most of your wonderful life.

Connect with me at:
www.facebook.com/donnaonthebeach and
www.twitter.com/donnaonthebeach

Also by Donna Higton

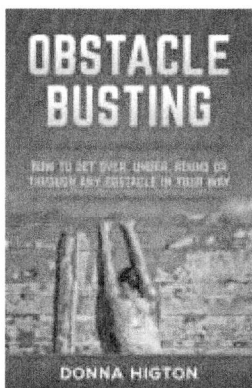

OBSTACLE BUSTING

HOW TO GET OVER, UNDER, ROUND OR THROUGH ANY OBSTACLE IN YOUR WAY

DONNA HIGTON

What is getting in the way of you living your best life?

We all come up against so many obstacles in our lives – from self-doubt to impatience, from getting stuck to having no time, from negativity to fear. These obstacles can stop you in your tracks, making you feel that you're not cut out for making your dreams come true or achieving your life goals. BUT obstacles are not there to stop you...they're there for you to get over, under, round and through so you can change your life.

This book will teach you:
• Why obstacles are a good thing
• Donna's top 4 obstacle busting tools
• How to get over, under, round and through 40+ common obstacles
• That you are not alone, or defective, or on the wrong path if you hit an obstacle

Obstacle Busting covers common obstacles such as comparisonitis, resistance, low self-esteem, worrying, having no money, not knowing what to do, biting off more than you can chew, getting stuck in an ebb, failure. If you're feeling stuck this book will show you how you overcome all your obstacles so you can make your dreams come true and change your life.

Over a decade of coaching clients to follow their dreams, and more than 15 years of following her own dreams, Donna has met every one of these obstacles...and overcome them all (some more than once). In this book, she shows you how to do the same so that nothing can get in the way of you living your most fabulous life.

Available now on Amazon.

Printed in Great Britain
by Amazon